"Now, more than ever, is the time to honest consideration of what is. Reading the work sister Syl within the pages of *Aphro-ism* will build the perfect foundation needed for activists or anyone wanting to end the oppression of all, by not being the oppressor of one."—**Seba Johnson**, Olympian, activist, and vegan since birth

"Aph and Syl Ko's work has deeply changed my views on activism for the animals. Every time, their work is eye-opening, revisiting the connections between animal liberation and human liberation in a way that is as much critical as constructive and inspiring."—**Frédéric Côté-Boudreau**, Québec-based activist, scholar, and blogger.

"*Aphro-ism* is an important read for anyone who is interested in thinking critically and wants to help to not only challenge but change the current dynamic of race and animals in our society. Thanks to these brilliant women of color, I've gained a new understanding of systems of oppression and feel less alone in the fight for social justice."—**lauren Ornelas**, Founder/Executive Director, Food Empowerment Project

"The Ko sisters are miles ahead of even the most progressive thinkers, with *Aphro-ism* establishing a theoretical framework and #BlackVegansRock demonstrating its practicability. There's no better metaphor for the failures of white supremacist capitalism than mortar, since it is the white slime that holds stone together. When the mortar cracks the whole building falls apart. Aph and Syl Ko are the stone. Crack them a thousand times and they remain unbroken."—**Rich Goldstein**, Producer, *The Daily Beast*

"Aph and Syl's anti-racist and anti-speciesist framework shifts the paradigm of nonhuman and human liberation. *Aphro-ism* is a revolutionary tool for holistic anti-oppression work that can benefit both grassroots activists and academic scholars."—**Raffaella Ciavatta**, Cofounder, Collectively Free, and activist

"Aph and Syl Ko are incredible activists and revolutionary thinkers who have influenced the way we approach animal rights and anti-racist activism. *Aphro-ism* has taught us to view oppression and liberation through a much clearer lens."—**David and Paige Carter**, Co-CEOs and Cofounders, The 300-Pound Vegan

"Syl Ko provides a crucial perspective to the movements seeking to secure rights for humans and nonhumans alike. As she so eloquently demonstrates, we should not treat human beings like 'animals' any more than we should treat animals like 'animals.' Syl's scholarship challenges us to reassess the standing social order and work toward a more just world."—**Steven M. Wise**, Founder and President, The Nonhuman Rights Project

"*Aphro-ism* is a groundbreaking suite of original essays on the entanglements of race, empire, gender, and species. In their analyses of human and animal oppression, Aph and Syl Ko deliver the trifecta: scholarship that is rigorous, accessible, and deeply important."—**Jason Wyckoff**, PhD

"Aph and Syl's brilliant work is laying the groundwork for an exciting new millennial generation of deeply critical and compassionate thinkers, feminists, and activists. *Aphro-ism* is helping countless young, hungry critical thinkers navigate through a world of 'isms,' make sense of endless contradictions, and come out the other side as more well-equipped, effective, woke activists."—**Richard Bowie**, editor at *VegNews* magazine

"*Aphro-ism* is paradigm-shattering! Whether your social justice lens leans single-issue or multi-issue, these essays offer razor-sharp critiques of hierarchical foundations and systemic oppression, while also providing frameworks for broad-scale liberation. This book is a vital companion for anyone willing to challenge surface-level 'connections' theories in exchange for deep, nuanced insights that have stratospheric potential for creating a more just world."—**Dawn Moncrief**, founder, A Well-Fed World

"Aph and Syl Ko have opened my eyes and my mind to the connection between ethical veganism and anti-racism activism. They never fail to inspire and blow my mind with their critical analysis on race and animality."—**Jenné Claiborne**, vegan chef, Sweet Potato Soul

"With *Aphro-ism*, Aph and Syl Ko have added their profound and revolutionary voices to a tradition of critical thinking around liberation, veganism, animal rights, anti-racism, and feminism. This is a sumptuous and necessary read that deepens the conversation and, most importantly, offers another way forward."—**Tracye McQuirter**, MPH, author of *By Any Greens Necessary*

APHRO-ISM

*Essays on Pop Culture, Feminism,
and Black Veganism from Two Sisters*

→ Aph Ko and Syl Ko ←

Lantern Books ● New York
A Division of Booklight Inc.

2017
Lantern Books
128 2nd Place
Brooklyn, NY 11231-4102
www.lanternbooks.com

Printed in the United States of America.

Library of Congress Cataloging
Publication information is available
upon request.

We dedicate this book to those who are committed to creating new conceptual architecture for the future. We hope this text serves as one of the bricks for the foundation.

CONTENTS

AUTHORS' NOTES

Aph Ko

THE SEEDS FOR *APHRO-ISM* WERE PLANTED A LONG TIME AGO, ALTHOUGH I was not able to cultivate what was trying to grow until 2015. *Aphro-ism* began as a website that I decided to launch after being fatigued with guest blogging on websites that other people owned. I've been blogging for over five years, and throughout all of that time, I wanted to create my own digital space. I'd always assumed that I had to use someone else's website as a vehicle to share my thoughts. I started to feel bored with how compartmentalized mainstream blogging sites were becoming. I wanted to offer a space that was dynamic, that tackled the deep entanglements of oppression, and simultaneously offered ways of moving closer toward liberation without privileging page clicks or compromising the analysis for vapid visibility. As a person of color who holds decolonial[1] sensibilities, I felt like I didn't really fit into any movement at all; therefore, I knew that I needed to carve out my own space.

I called my older sister Syl, seeking her encouragement to make my own website. I vividly remember how nervous I was, because I didn't feel I had the strength to create the space I wanted, especially because I knew it would be controversial. With controversy comes responsibility, and I didn't know if I had the emotional energy to deal with the digital baggage. With Syl's support, I moved forward with my plan. I decided on the name "Aphro-ism" because it sounds like *aphorism*, a truth. An additional bonus was that my name was already integrated into it. I specifically emphasized the "ism" in the title because I knew the site would be dedicated to interrogating "isms" in popular culture.

Syl and I have always had a close relationship, which I have treasured. When I was seventeen years old, Syl introduced me to radical books by Angela Davis, W. E. B. Du Bois, and George Jackson. For over ten years, Syl and I have challenged each other intellectually and we have written emails to one another about feminism, anti-racism, and animal rights. Some of the biggest shifts in my political opinions have occurred after intense conversations with her. Naturally, I asked her if she wanted to write for my new digital space. She agreed to contribute and we started compiling what we had. We used our various backgrounds in media studies, women's studies, philosophy, and critical race theory to create short essays that challenged dominant ways of thinking about social justice topics. We didn't just stick to one topic either—we explored it all. We had no idea that so many people were going to read our work. In fact, we used to joke that *no one* would ever read our work since it was so weird and different.

In less than seven months, we started picking up major traffic on our website and we were nominated for a 2016 *VegNews* magazine Bloggy Award, which was a pretty big deal considering our controversial writing crossed the lines that were neatly drawn around compartmentalized activist movements. Authors and activists from all around the world reached out to tell us how much our work had influenced their own, and to this day we are always shocked and humbled to read these messages.

Syl and I unapologetically wrote our thoughts about veganism, anti-racism, feminism, and popular culture on Aphro-ism, the website. We did this for seven to eight months before we realized just how much of a resource Aphro-ism could be, especially as a book. In particular, I remember being contacted by *several* black and brown vegans who were looking for a book that discussed the issues Syl and I wrote on the website. Literature can revolutionize a movement and I felt there weren't many books that discussed these complex topics (decolonial theory, animality, anti-racism, movement politics) in an accessible way, and we wanted to fill that gap.

As life started getting busier, and as different projects came our way, we realized we couldn't keep up with the demands of the website in the ways that we wanted. We knew that the literature we provided on the site was valuable, so we decided to turn it into a book. We took our most popular essays (with the addition of some new, unpublished ones), edited them, and compiled them for you here. Some essays explicitly deal with veganism; others explore popular culture and feminism. We include a range of subjects that reflect our interests and passions.

On a political note, we also wanted to trouble the ways that we're allowed to write about controversial *contemporary* subjects. Blogging can sometimes feel hollow: you have to write something quickly to stay relevant, which can compromise the analysis. We wanted to slow down and really focus our thoughts. We wanted to read different perspectives, sit with other people's writings for a while, and feel challenged, which blogging didn't really accommodate, since everything is so fast-paced. Since we were addressing controversial topics in a new way, we also wanted to honor the complexities by not publishing everything immediately online.

Although blogging has been an outlet for me for years, I started to feel uneasy about the overall landscape of the online world, and I began to realize that blogging about these profoundly complex issues might not be such a good idea. The online world is ripe with exploitation, co-optation, and harassment, particularly for minorities. When I started to receive more mainstream attention for my work, the negative feedback increased because my words were taken out of context, or one or two sentences from an interview would go viral that didn't accurately reflect my politics or my theories. Because people already have a narrow idea of what "veganism" or "racism" looks like (thanks to our one-dimensional mainstream media culture), I knew the deck was already stacked against those trying to rearticulate the relationships between racism and nonhuman animal oppression. The preconceived notions surrounding the conversation usually trumped the words I wrote.

In other words, people who did not regularly engage with literature that centered on racism through a lens of animality didn't have the necessary tools to engage with our work. Some writers for mainstream websites criticized my articles, relegating my words to the sphere of activists who merely *compared* black oppression to animal oppression without understanding that most of my work denounces that practice. This was exemplified most thoroughly in November 2016, when Black Entertainment Television (BET) published an article about me titled, "Black Feminist Dragged for Comparing Meat-Eating to White Supremacy." This made me realize that most folks in the mainstream react strongly to my work because of the preexisting conversation about animal oppression. Because *some* white folks compared black oppression to nonhuman animal oppression, a lot of people immediately assumed I was doing that too, only because I talked about white supremacy and animality. I knew that providing nuance and context through a book was necessary in order to gain control of the message and to de-center white-centric campaigns that normally came to people's minds when *anyone* talked about blackness and animality. In other words, I was getting tired of paying the cost for some white people fucking up the conversation.

I took a break from blogging to reassess what my next steps should be in terms of regaining control of the narrative. I wanted to unplug and focus on my thoughts for a little so I could present them in a way that made sense, because these issues are important and they deserve to be presented in a manner that reflects their complexity.

I also wanted to create something tangible, something you can hold and feel connected with, especially in a society that is so emotionally disconnected. I love a really challenging book I can sit on my bed with and read when I feel isolated or when I feel I'm the only one in the world who is thinking a certain way. A good book can change your life, and I sincerely hope that this book changes yours, especially those of you who feel you don't fit in with any of the current movements.

We want you to enjoy these essays, and we ask you to keep an open mind as you explore each one. Syl and I specifically wrote this book in a style that reflects our politics—we don't write in one way, all of the essays are different lengths, and we don't stick to one topic. There isn't one linear narrative in this, and we like it that way because it reflects the way we have conversations together.

Some articles are more academic whereas others are filled with plain, unapologetic rage. We also employ humor to help us navigate complex issues. We want this book to read like an intellectual journal between two sisters, because that is really how Syl and I treated Aphro-ism the website. Many of our essays were produced after hours of talking over the phone, discussing the political issues of the day. We left the original dates under each essay title so you can see when these thoughts were published on the website. We are doing this so you can witness our political and intellectual growth over time. You might even see contradictions between our earlier and later essays, which we would argue isn't a bad thing. Too often in this society, we prize and celebrate people for never changing their minds. We're trained to view change as a sign of weakness, an idea that we want to trouble. We celebrate growth, and we wanted that to be a part of this book.

I decided to name this book *Aphro-ism: Essays on Pop Culture, Feminism, and Black Veganism from Two Sisters* specifically because I am still interrogating each of these words and cultural spaces. I have a complicated relationship with popular culture, feminism, *and* black veganism. In this book, we question them because we are still sincerely grappling with them ourselves.

The reality is that Syl and I are just two people trying to make sense of what's around us in the best way we know how. We are not experts, nor are we here to tell you how you *should* view the world. This collection of essays demonstrates where we're trying to work out our frustrations and confusion, our ideas and hopes, and our suggestions for a better, more empathetic world. This isn't an end point to our thoughts, either. I'm sure as we read and discuss more, we'll extend these conversations and even continue to change our minds, because activism is all about growth and learning, never staying in the same conceptual space for too long.

Syl and I have been communicating with each other for over a decade about critical concepts, and this book is a glimpse into our conversations. We hope you enjoy it.

Syl Ko

Lots of people might laugh if one were to say that eating meat/eggs/dairy or going to be entertained/learn at the zoo is *racist*. But that's because race and racism have been framed as phenomena linked only to skin color, the body, or geo-specificity. Race encompasses much more than our limited discourse allows. Race is broad. Race is vague. It hovers over and infects every aspect of our lives, whether or not we notice. Not only are people and groups raced, but so are regions, so are all members of the environment, so is knowledge, so is language, so is time and space itself. Some might think I'm exaggerating when I say this. They say, "Oh, you just want to make everything about race." Not quite. What I am saying is that race is about everything.

Although I have been obsessed with the "animal question" for as long as I can remember, and have been through every phase an animal rights advocate could have gone through, it did not occur to me that the question was one that had to be examined along with the question about race until I reread Aimé Césaire's *Discourse on Colonialism*. I struggled with his claim that the Negro had been "an invention of Europe." Obviously, European colonialism did not *materially* create dark-skinned human beings whom they referred to as Negroes and planted throughout the African continent. Rather, Césaire was pointing to a *conceptual* invention that was foisted onto Africans (and those descended from Africa) and that served to govern the different ways that Europeans were meant to think of them and how Africans were to think of themselves. It would not have mattered if Africans excelled at all of the same tasks, rational and otherwise, which Europeans did, or if they possessed identical attributes, skills, or properties. Their belonging to the category "Negro" *all by itself* locks black people into an inferior social status from which they cannot escape as long as categories like these continue to thrive.

I began to model a view of animal oppression using this idea that the category *animal* was also a colonial invention that has been imposed on humans and animals. As I began to reread and discover literature that belongs to a long, beautiful anti-/decolonial tradition of investigating our notions of "humanity" and "the human," I realized that the category *animal* that continues to disadvantage actual animals also operates in human oppressions, particularly racialized oppressed groups. It struck me as odd, though, that despite the huge volume of literature in this tradition that grasped the racialized nature of the category *the human* and the animalization of humans as a means to exploit, violate, and/or eliminate them, there was not much serious consideration of actual nonhuman animals or how this project of racialization affected *them*.

My contributions to *Aphro-ism* take up this very matter. I do not claim to be saying anything particularly original and I try my best to make it clear that I am informed by and building on a very long tradition of black and brown thinkers, activists, scholars, citizen-intellectuals, and artists who have, from the beginning, seen the human–animal binary in effect in racial oppression. My admittedly narrow focus is to apply this tradition of radical thought to an overlooked but obvious question—that of the animal—and to see what comes of it.

I don't want to give the impression that I arbitrarily chose Césaire as a place to start thinking about animals. We use the word *radical*, but even the radical literature concerning race that examines the *invention* of the human—such as that by Césaire, Frantz Fanon, and Sylvia Wynter—fails to mention how the simultaneous invention of "the animal" might pull on us to make us question our attitudes toward animals in the black community. As I argue in several of my essays, transforming and resignifying one will most definitely require transforming and resignifying the other.

Similarly, in animal rights spaces, there is a lot of talk about being "radical," but I do not think animal rights advocates or theorists realize just *how* radical a venture it is to morally accommodate animals. We can't just borrow mainstream ways of thinking to undo the present moral order. We can't simply *include* animals within the established, diseased framework. Animal advocates are willing to break into laboratories, kick in car windows, march through popular restaurants and stores chanting and telling the stories of animals, and will stand outside in the freezing cold as "radical" measures to resist and challenge the widespread (ab)use of animals. But few actually have been radical enough to change how they think. It is not enough merely to realize that animals suffer and that they deserve better. We have to wrap our heads around *the modes of thinking* that were designed precisely to ensure certain humans, animals, and other nonhuman life remain outside our moral and social communities. This is not a precious, academic, intellectual activity. This is absolutely necessary for real change. I am hoping animal advocates see our essays as an offering—as at least one potential way *truly* to radicalize their movement.

FOREWORD

I HAVE BEEN FAMILIAR WITH THE RADICAL, BRILLIANT, AND INNOVATIVE scholarship of Aph and Syl Ko for several years now. Their blog, Aphro-ism, has been one of the best feminist and critical race approaches to justice (that includes pro-vegan frameworks) that I have ever encountered. The sibling duo is the epitome of decolonial thought within the spheres of critical animal studies, critical race studies, Black Studies, and feminism.

Aphro-ism comes to us at crucial moments in time: (1) An era when US mainstream animal liberation continues to be deeply challenged with moving beyond one-dimensional, often "post-racial" approaches to justice and freedom for nonhuman animals; (2) the continuation of black liberation, particularly through the Black Lives Matter movement and; (3) a Trump presidential administration that has frighteningly revealed how nearly fifty percent of the United States desires to "Make America Great Again" by rescinding civil, reproductive, and human rights, denying climate change, and repealing environmental protection policies and acts (to name a few) . . . all to lead us back into the days of Jim Crow or even antebellum chattel slavery. Within all of these pivotal moments, the Ko sisters have brilliantly and bravely written how both the taken-for-granted mainstream concepts of *animality, whiteness,* and *race* are intertwined and rooted in this country's over-four-hundred-year-old white supremacist racial caste, speciesist, and capitalist systems.

This book challenges the popular narrative that anti-speciesism and Black Liberation/anti-racism are all incompatible with, and divisive toward, each other. Most notably, this trope of "divisiveness" has been regurgitated within white-dominated animal liberation and vegan spaces for decades. This myth that (white racialized) consciousness produces "objective, "universal," and "raceless" knowledge about nonhuman animals is dismantled, deconstructed, and decentered within *Aphro-ism*.

Within these pages, the Ko sisters embark on an adventure of epistemic justice to unhinge normative whiteness from the taken-for-granted center, replacing it with a black feminist scholarly and embodied praxis to achieve multiple forms of justice and resistance. Their innovative literary journey asks two fundamental questions: (1) How do animal liberation and veganism inform (and are informed by) the USA's racial caste system? and (2) What is the potential for black liberation and anti-racism movements when anti-speciesism is critically integrated without erasing blackness (as both political identity and collective epistemology)? Without apology (and they should not need to apologize), the Ko sisters make it clear that their decolonial approaches to anti-racism, animal liberation, and other forms of justice will not pander to the emotional needs of the "post-racial" white status quo within the animal liberation movement and beyond.

Furthermore, like many vegans of color doing justice work for nonhuman animals and human beings, Syl and Aph critically but compassionately narrate their challenges in being anti-racist and black feminist scholars amongst people of color who do not politicize animality. The Ko sisters convey how some non-white nonvegans misunderstand the sisters' commitment to animal liberation as equating nonhuman animals as *the same as* black people— a controversial and triggering topic for many, but necessary to address and unpack if more progress is to be made for all beings. It is the unique path of addressing *animality*—not necessarily animal liberation—through which Aph and Syl brilliantly broach and unpack this volatile dialogue. Let go what you think you may know about black feminism, anti-racism, and animal liberation. Come and embark on a journey with these two game-changers to alter the future of feminism, racial justice, ethics, and veganism.

Dr. A. Breeze Harper
April 2017

BLACK LIVES, BLACK LIFE

◆

Syl Ko
August 10, 2015

IN THIS CHAPTER, I WANT TO DISCUSS AND CONNECT TWO SEEMINGLY disparate conversations: one concerning diversity and the other concerning #blacklivesmatter. There's a troubling aspect present in both, and that is the interpretation of blackness or brownness as essentially *bodied*. In other words, the mainstream (read: white) tendency to find us visible insofar as we are regarded merely as bodies is a tendency that we have internalized and one that we now perpetuate in our own movements.

I'm not trying to pull any philosophical lingo on you by using the term *bodied*. I don't mean to say there is something problematic about our having bodies. Also, I don't think there is anything inferior about bodies or that they "drag down" our existence or any other such nonsense. Understanding beings as "bodied" becomes a problem when beings are viewed *primarily* in terms of their bodies. That is, reducing conscious, active beings with viewpoints, interests, and/or projects—*subjects*—into merely the biological frame that houses the source of this activity—*objects*—is destructive to those beings. Time after time, this type of reduction is used to justify horrendous treatment. The phenomena of slavery, human experimentation, sex camps, human exhibits in zoos, etc., were made possible by interpreting these beings as primarily bodied. And the phenomena of slaughtering nonhumans for meat, the gross manipulation of female nonhuman reproductive capacities for dairy and egg production, scientific experimentation on nonhumans, the incarceration of nonhumans in zoos, etc., are also made possible by pretending these beings are best understood as merely bodied.

My task in this chapter isn't to beg white people to drop this interpretation of black people. My aim is to make us reflect on ways in which people of color may have internalized this interpretation of ourselves, especially in activist spaces, and how to move away from that interpretation.

The #blacklivesmatter movement is one obvious place to turn. Although the slogan demands that black *lives* matter, some of us are upset that black *deaths* don't seem to matter. If you don't believe me, take a look at our community's reaction to the way mainstream news outlets reported the death of Cecil the lion—whom a white Minnesotan killed on a trophy hunt in Zimbabwe. Of course, in saying that our deaths matter, we are in a roundabout way saying our lives matter. But what do we mean when we say our "lives" matter?

Given the context in which the slogan was born, there is overwhelming attention to and emphasis on the biological aspect of black life. Black people are violently targeted, tortured, and murdered left and right, many times in the light of day. But even though these unjust attacks on black bodies have helped to make this issue a mainstream one, the myopic focus on actual or biological black life and death is just reproducing the black-as-bodied narrative. The framing of the issue in this biological way puts at stake the way we believe we can move forward or "do something" about this problem.

For instance, obsessive and excessive attention has been devoted to the issue of police violence. Some may think I'm being harsh in calling what seems to be deserved focus "obsessive and excessive," but let's face it: we in the black community have always had a disastrous relationship with the police. Just because white people are beginning to trust our word on this doesn't merit hitching every solution to investigating the police or installing cameras or trying to make fair the inherently racist justice system. That's not to say these are all bad ideas. I'm merely saying these aren't necessarily ways to move forward. Some of us who are a little more seasoned might even agree with George Jackson when he wrote: "How ridiculous we must seem to the rest of the black world when we beg the government to investigate their own protective agencies."[1]

The particular framework in which we cast these types of solutions is restrictive because the interpretation of the problem that underpins this framework is itself restrictive. Yes, black people's actual, biological lives and bodies are under attack. But what if we go deeper to find what is giving rise to this phenomenon? This requires seeing the problem as more than just physical violation . . . and seeing ourselves as beyond primarily bodied.

One way I suggest construing the issue is as follows: symbolic or cultural elimination of black Life is a necessary condition for which literal elimination of black lives is made possible. We've been so focused on biological black "lives" that we have lost sight of what might be a cause of this problem: the routine dismissal of black Life. Life (capital L) is more than biological. Life includes those activities that make life worth living and valuable; it is what lends *weight* to our existence as human beings. To feel alive, to have a life that feels worthy of living, to experience one's "weight" as a living subject is not merely to feel one's pulse or possess a working brain. It's something more.

The ways in which we as humans construct Life for ourselves usually demand an ongoing dialogue with the world in which we exist. These dialogues manifest themselves as contributions that attempt to engage with society; art, music, film, science, religion, theory, literature, and philosophy are some categories in which these conversations occur. Other times, Life can be constructed by ongoing dialogues with microworlds we have created for ourselves, such as our families or communities, and these are usually represented or treated in art, music, film, theory, etc.

The problem is that we live in a society (and world, for that matter) that either erases, or rejects, or diminishes the value of contributions offered by black people; which then entails the erasure, rejection, or inferiorization of family and community life represented and treated in many of those contributions. In other words, we live in a society that culturally or symbolically eliminates black Life. We might even call it a US tradition:

black Life does not matter. If it did, then we'd not still find ourselves drowning in whiteness and Eurocentricity to this day.

It is here that the discussion thus far links up well with the second conversation I mentioned at the beginning: diversity. We can find the black-as-bodied narrative in operation here as well; in many ways, it fuels the US tradition of erasing or rejecting black Life. In short, diversity (or rather "diversity") is the idea that black (and brown) people should function as vessels for white perspectives and white theory as opposed to contributing their own viewpoints and theories. The assumption here is that the considerations of black people are either inferior or negligible and so the value of black people in any space will be in their ability to reproduce whiteness. In simpler words, "diversity" is the *presence of black bodies*, as opposed to the presence of black ideas born from black perspectives, in predominantly white spaces.

Let's look at two examples that demonstrate how we fall into this way of thinking:

(1) Many times, people—including black people—think they are "being diverse" when they choose to focus on some type of project that concentrates on an issue that affects non-white people or makes non-white people the prime subjects of the project. More often than not, the *framework* from which the study or research project is generated is Eurocentric. Just because the project is "about race," or concerns black and brown people, does not mean you are valuing diversity. Valuing diversity in such a context means recognizing that theoretical models devised by brown and black people, *especially those that directly challenge Eurocentricity*, are just as good, if not even more appropriate, to frame your research projects or studies in, whether or not they are about black or brown populations.

(2) Now let's consider an example that touches on "strategies for inclusion" in spaces that find it difficult to recruit black people.

As a student in philosophy, I can speak to this example from experience: all across the US, faculties in philosophy programs are scrambling for ways to "get black people interested in philosophy." in order to do something about the abysmal number of non-whites, particularly black people, in the profession. I am depressed to say I know more than a handful of black philosophers who are enthusiastically invested in this "project" as well. Of course, the truth is black people have been philosophizing all along, but "top" programs refuse to acknowledge those works as "real" philosophy. So, the problem isn't some mysterious malaise affecting black people that prevents them from appreciating the virtues of philosophy and applying to philosophy programs. The problem is that the white gatekeepers of philosophical inquiry maintain a particularly Eurocentric conception of "philosophy."

What's especially poignant with diversity rhetoric is that black people are being used to erase our *own* perspectives. You can see why Aph and I reject the idea that any of this is actual diversity. We call it "cosmetic diversity": be black, think white. Others call it "imperial diversity." Angela Davis describes it as "a corporate strategy."[2]

It seems that cosmetic diversity is itself *adding* to the problem of disappearing black lives given that this flawed understanding of diversity seeks to reject genuine contributions from black people for the sake of upholding and glorifying white ones. If physical erasure of black people is made possible by our cultural or symbolic erasure, and "diversity" functions to include our black bodies in white spaces but rejects our unique perspectives, then "diversity" is not on our side.

This lack of interest in black Life and the activity of erasing our contributions, voices, and perspectives play a central role in making possible our physical, literal erasure. If the very thing that makes us "really alive"—the contributions that make our existence possible and worthwhile as social beings—is regarded as nonexistent, pointless, inferior, or not worth even acknowledging, then we have already been killed. If our artistic vision, our theoretical endeavors, our constructs are completely without value and have no place in the world, mere flesh and blood will never persuade anyone that we have a rightful place here. What exactly are the grounds to prove that our lives matter when our Life doesn't matter to the world at large?

So, how do we move forward? Well, we have to take black Life seriously. But to do that, we first have to look backward to our brothers and sisters in the struggle who pointed out a long time ago that *black lives are not supposed to matter*. We were never *meant* to be on equal footing with white people. This is what Aimé Césaire means when he describes the "Negro" as "an invention of Europe."[3] As black people, we are *supposed* to be inferior in precisely this way. People of any race can understand that surely black biological life matters: killing or beating black people is wrong. People of any race can understand that surely black bodies should be included in all spaces. Excluding black people from places is wrong. But this does not mean those people understand that black Life matters. And this does not mean that those people understand that black ideas and perspectives should be welcome in all spaces. You can be a diehard activist, shutting down highways with your protests against police killings, and still be a part of the problem if you fail to take seriously black art, black theory, black perspectives. You can be the president of the committee on diversity and still be an enemy to true diversity if your only concern is to recruit black and brown bodies instead of black and brown ideas.

We have to be careful in how we prod our allies (and ourselves) to action on these issues. If we maintain the current strategy, we might—at most—get mainstream society to care about us when we're dead. How about we try to get society to care about us, *really* care about us, while we're alive?

BRINGING OUR DIGITAL MOPS HOME
A Call to Black Folks to Stop Cleaning up
White Folks' Intellectual Messes Online

◆

Aph Ko
August 12, 2015

AFTER POPULAR BLACK FEMINIST COMEDIAN AND VIDEO BLOGGER AKILAH Hughes released "On Intersectionality in Feminism and Pizza," a video that went viral on YouTube, social justice websites and magazines enthusiastically promoted the video for weeks. Hughes created the video to explain to white women why white feminism[1] inherently excludes women of color, and she offers intersectional feminism as a more appropriate framework to help bring about the liberation of all women. In Hughes' video, men are symbolized through burgers, and women are symbolized through pizza. Cheese pizza represents white women and deluxe pizza (with sausage and peppers) represents any combination of minoritized[2] identities (like being transgender, disabled, and/or of color). Hughes employs humor to demonstrate how difficult it is to navigate a "burger's world" as *any* type of pizza; however, she specifically highlights how it's particularly difficult for deluxe pizzas.[3]

Hughes educates the viewer about intersectionality and oppression, however, when she holds up the burgers and pizzas to the camera, it becomes evident that the animal products she uses as props will not be factored into her analysis on oppression.

Frankly, it was not surprising that Hughes did not problematize her use of animal products in the video (to be fair, animal products weren't the focus of her message), nor does she examine animal oppression in her regular advocacy. However, what I saw in Hughes' viral video was representative of what I regularly saw in the mainstream landscape of black anti-racist activism: a focus on publicly educating individual white people coupled with the routine dismissal of animal oppression.

The public celebration of Hughes' video reminded me of how I felt when I saw the mainstream black community's response to Cecil the lion. *Clutch*, an online magazine dedicated to progressive, hip, young black women, published an article called "Maybe People Should Dress Like Lions, or How Cecil the Lion Has Gotten More Sympathy than Dead Black People."[4] The author writes about the ways the mainstream white public quickly organized around Cecil in hopes of bringing justice, yet remained silent when black people were killed at the hands of police. In the *New York Times*, well-known black feminist Roxane Gay wrote, "A late-night television host did not cry on camera this week for human lives that have been lost. He certainly doesn't have to. He did, however, cry for a lion and that's worth thinking about."[5]

This overt centering of white people's reactions to black death in the media has produced a type of "Dear White People"[6] syndrome within black activism, where black folks spend their time and energy writing posts to white people, creating educational videos for white people about racism, and spending all of their energy debating white people online. This has actually given rise to a phenomenon called "Racial Discussion Fatigue Syndrome."[7]

Some of the most visible mainstream anti-racist activism manifests itself through teaching white people how they are racist, where their privileges are located, and what they can do to "be better." I'm reminded of a popular video that came out on *Huffington Post*, featuring Zeba Blay, a black writer. "Why We Need to Talk about White Feminism"[8] essentially explains to white women the problems with their advocacy. The video also features a white woman alongside Blay who helps in educating the presumed white viewer. The problem with this type of activism is that it positions black people as automatic racial experts who explain racism to white people, and it casts individual white people as the problem. This was most evident with our community's reaction to Cecil, where mainstream black activists intervened to publicly discipline white people for emotionally catering to a dead nonhuman animal. This was typified through a satirical tweet by Roxane Gay: "I'm personally going to start wearing a lion costume when I leave my house so if I get shot, people will care."[9]

Of course, I understand why some minoritized people respond this way. Black people are undergoing systemic violence; therefore, our physical experiences with racism can take precedence over other issues. Additionally, when the mainstream white public focuses on nonhuman animals, beings our Western society labels automatically *less than* and, thus, disposable, it's seen as the ultimate of disrespectful, racial acts.

However, I have always argued that we, as minoritized people, should include the violence that nonhuman animals receive in *our* theoretical anti-racist frameworks because it's a more complex way of understanding the systems that are impacting us as people of color. As black folks, we have been encouraged to create borders around our own racial oppression without realizing that white supremacy provides us with those border walls to ensure that we never fully see how complex our oppression really is.[10] The walls have been so high that we haven't been able to see that our struggle involves the struggle of others; and since we can't see the massive landscape of white supremacy beyond this barrier, we don't realize just how expansive its territory is.

Rather than fighting the system of white supremacy, we spend time "calling out" individual white people and/or white news media. The little energy we have left after dealing with internalized racism and systemic oppression is spent on fighting and educating white people.

Normally, the conversation gets turned to the ways that white folks in the animal rights landscape have no regard for the racist violence inflicted on black people. Although that's a legitimate conversation that is currently being written and talked about extensively, as black folks we need to realize that an important conversation lurks under all this mess that *we* need to be having among ourselves as well.

The mainstream black community's reaction to Cecil made me realize that, as black people, we have spent way too much time worrying about white people and educating them. When we privilege educating or fighting individual white people *as* anti-racist activism, we lose sight of the structure that is causing us violence and we subscribe to a simplistic version of how the system works. Our energy might be better spent on examining just how expansive the territory of white supremacy is, which may lead us to understand that white supremacy is much more complex than the actions of individual white people.

We need to stop serving as intellectual maids to white people, cleaning up their privileged white messes by writing articles and creating videos to help them get back on track. While we've been helping white people clean up their intellectual homes for free, ours have begun to collect dust.

Black folks are committed to having racial conversations with white people, a commitment that speaks to our resilience and strength during an era where some of us are just trying to survive. However, sometimes we forget that racial work as a community requires us to be critical of our own ways, too, including our conceptual frameworks. We have work to do *within* our own movements and this will require us to engage seriously and dialogue with the different and diverse black social justice movements. *Black folks aren't monolithic, and neither are our movements to overturn white supremacy.*

For example, I thought it was odd that during the Cecil debates, mainstream black news sites and well-trafficked black websites didn't appear (at least to my knowledge) to reach out to black vegans to get their viewpoints or to gain some new insight within the context of anti-racism and animality. Instead, they immediately focused on white people's reactions to the event. This is a problem. In fact, I have noticed that whenever it comes to veganism or animal oppression, the loudest voices on these topics in the black community are people who *aren't* vegan, and don't talk or write about animal oppression at all, which is problematic. Although some nonvegan black folks point to the ways that white folks animalize them, this argument isn't necessarily the same as talking about nonhuman animal oppression. Some of these folks have not yet been exposed to the idea of animality as a racialized weapon of white supremacy. Rather than immediately engage with white people's reactions to events, which will inevitably lead to conversations about the racial insensitivity of individual white people, it might be beneficial for us to privilege diverse perspectives in our own communities.

In the black community, to speak of "the animal" is to highlight generations' worth of anxieties about our own identities, as well as the oppressive conditions of white supremacy. However, we can't afford to shy away from conversations with each other that could advance our own causes.

Unfortunately, the implicit assumption is that black vegans are the same as white ones, privileging animal experiences over black human experiences. Neither could be further from the truth. Most black vegans I have encountered place anti-racism at the center of their activism. I'm reminded of a time when black lawyers protested an event at which I was speaking on a panel with another black vegan activist and a white vegan lawyer. The black lawyers reportedly said the event shouldn't spotlight "self-hating blacks" (meaning black people who were advocating for black liberation alongside animal liberation). They assumed I was going to be playing into the tropes of white veganism by "comparing" oppressions to draw sympathy with animal oppression.

As it happened, the title of my talk was, "Beyond Victim Comparisons: Creating a New Vocabulary for White Human Terrorism." Ironically, my talk centered on the ways that we *shouldn't* compare black oppression to animal oppression because they aren't "like" each other; they just have a common source of oppression, which is systemic white human violence. Unfortunately, some of the critics didn't attend the event, which made me realize the power of white people's framing of these conversations, since they can control how minoritized people will even engage with the subject. As black folks, we must push past the ways individual white people have constructed the conversation to foreground our *own* experiences and perspectives. Currently, we, as black activists, are positioned as perpetual racial experts with a fixed experience and manner of viewing our own conditions. This prevents us from examining the different means by which our oppression is sustained.

Liberatory social change will require us, as minorities, to change our thinking as well. If we know that racism and sexism are systemic issues that impact *everyone*, why would we think that white people are the only ones who need to reevaluate their behaviors and conceptual frameworks? The system has infected us all. It is illogical to talk about "structures" in one breath, and then have our advocacy structured around disciplining *individual* white people. Liberation will require *all of us* to act differently and to reevaluate how we've been trained to understand what the actual problems are, and their solutions. Change won't just be an external event, but will happen internally as well. Liberation requires us to knock down the wall we've placed around our own oppression as black people so we can see the expansive territory of white supremacy and how it impacts many other marginalized groups.

So, I'm asking for us to return home with the digital mops we've been using online to clean up white people's intellectual messes, and start placing some of that attention on one another. This is an extension of self-care. Frequently, self-care is interpreted as an individualized phenomenon; however, I see it as a way of putting energy into our collective black selves. This certainly doesn't mean that we can't or shouldn't engage white people in conversations about their privilege. It simply means that that's not the only route to dismantling white supremacy.

→ 3 ←

#AllVegansRock
The All Lives Matter Hashtag of Veganism

◆

Aph Ko
August 19, 2015

In June 2015, I wrote the first article listing 100 Black Vegans.[1] I felt compelled to do this after I witnessed conversations from animal rights activists about the "whiteness" of the movement. There appeared to be a strong desire among activists to include representations of people of color in advocacy; however, I saw that people didn't necessarily have the right tools to move forward with this plan outside of hosting conversations about inclusivity and diversity.

I started to notice that diversity rhetoric *itself* was eclipsing contributions from vegans of color. In 2015, Dr. Amie Breeze Harper launched "The Vegan Praxis of Black Lives Matter,"[2] an online conference where vegans from different racial backgrounds analyzed the intersections between racism and speciesism. (Syl talks more about speciesism in chapter 17.) Unfortunately, this conference didn't get nearly as much attention as the nebulous conversations about "diversity." (Although the presence of vegans of color certainly doesn't negate the point that the racial grammar of the movement is white, the movement tends to highlight whiteness, rather than focus on the people of color already in the movement.)

I realized that with a simple paradigm shift, vegans could actualize our goals at making the mainstream animal rights movement racially diverse since, technically, it already was. Vegans of color were doing the work, but there wasn't any serious infrastructure in place to ensure they were receiving the visibility and support in the animal advocacy movement they deserved. I wanted to write an article listing black game-changers who were vegan, alongside black vegans who didn't identify as activists, to demonstrate how normalized plant-based eating was in many of our communities.

This was my way of showing *how* black lives matter. Not only would I be deconstructing white-centric mainstream animal rights spaces, but I'd also be reconstructing—offering something new instead of just criticizing.

When my article was published, vegans of color all over the world contacted me, appreciative of the list, honored to be on it, and wanting to be included in the project. Although the article was well received, some called it "racist" and "speciesist" because it apparently detracted from the goals of the animal rights movement. Such attacks were alarming; but they weren't surprising, considering black folks are usually called "segregationists" and "racists" when we attempt to carve out spaces of empowerment for ourselves.[3]

The Vegan Society shared my article on their Facebook page (which had over 300,000 followers at the time) and I was overwhelmed by the torrent of post-racial, racist, and offensive comments that followed.[4] I have included *some* (from the hundreds) of comments directed at my article, which merely sought to highlight black vegans who were working in the areas of food justice, animal rights, anti-racism, and feminism. (It must also be noted that vegans of color—particularly non-black minorities—also participated in writing racist comments under the article.)

I am not aiming to shock you, because these responses are somewhat predictable (especially if you've been in the movement for some time). However, I think it's necessary to document the anger directed at the 100 Black Vegans article as proof of black folks' claims that there is racism in the animal rights movement. These responses remind me of the misguided panic over Anita Sarkeesian's analysis of video games wherein people asked: *What does gender inequality have to do with video games?*[5] Similarly, folks below ask: *What does race have to do with the animals?*

You created a racial discussion and you derailed the purpose of veganism to further your cause.

It's just as racially exclusive to have a 100 black vegans list as it would be to have a 100 white vegans. Why is this acceptable? 100 just . . . vegans would be fine. Pretty sure the animals don't care what colour face they're not being shoveled into, why is this still so important to us? It's 2015.

Well done The Vegan Society, you just successfully created a racial discussion out of a topic which should be about diet and health, regardless of skin color.

It's a sad world when we have to bring the race issues into one's dietary habits.

Isn't this racist?

Can you imagine a "White Vegans Rock" post? No, I thought not.

We'll never have equality so long as people are praised for simply being _____ race. There are no black vegans, or white vegans, or red vegans, etc. There are only vegans.

There are no black vegans, white vegans, red vegans. . . . We are ALL vegans in brotherhood and sisterhood for the good of the environment, our beloved animals, and our own health. It seems to be the minority's [*sic*] communities who continually like to segregate that condemn white segregation. I am vegan with all who are vegan.

Why does EVERYTHING always have to be about race? Why can't it just simply be all about being a vegan, not about being a black vegan or a white vegan or an Asian vegan? Why label each other? This kind of thinking baffles me. It's exactly this kind of thinking that makes worldwide racism such a big issue.

I'M A NON-WHITE VEGAN, PAY ATTENTION TO ME INSTEAD OF THE BUTCHERED ANIMALS!!! Oh how lovely.

I completely do not understand why we have to have "lists." I am an Asian-American who happens to be vegan; I don't need to be acknowledged for my choice. I know I made it. There seems to be so much separation in unity. I am just happy to know there are vegans from many countries, many walks of life, and that we strive to make the world a better place—for animals and for humans.

If someone had made a list highlighting only white vegans, someone would have a tantrum over it. So why it's OK to make one of all black people is something many of us scratch our heads at.

I am going to unsub and unlike you, The Vegan Society—you are totally out to cause division. You are making vegans argue amongst themselves and the direction of their argument is miles away from being vegan. Donald [Watson, the cofounder of The Vegan Society] is rolling in his grave. I don't have time for people who cause division.

I get what you're saying yet I've never thought about vegans being black, white, or any other color. We are people. That's the bottom line.

I'm not following your site anymore. You are bringing sex, colour, whatever you can to promote veganism and all this is bullshit, it's about animals' death not art, colour, etc. Blimey, you guys certainly know how to complicate things. Thanks for nothing.

Why does it matter what color a vegan is? The fact remains that vegans of all colors are awesome.

My thought on this post as written: last I checked, vegans do not eat black people. That said, just because an organization does not make it a point to give the Black Lives Matter campaign a deliberate shout out does not mean there is no support.

I think it's ridiculous to just have one list. Do Caucasians, Asians, Hispanics, and mixed races not matter? Why not have lists of them? I think it best to have a list of vegans period. But if it helps a person of a specific race decide to become vegan because another person of the same race is vegan then it's good. I'm not going to bother reading your article because all lives matter.

Why?? Why put labels on people, black people, gay people, white people, short people, STOP PEOPLE. We are all the same!

Why does it always have to be about race? So sick of it all! Will you be featuring all people every month? White Vegans, Australian Vegans, Women Vegans, Handicap Vegans, Military Vegans?? See my point?

Veganism doesn't care what colour you are and no one should celebrate division unless you are racists anyway. No black, white, hetero, gay, transsexual, pink, fluffy or anything vegan. It's JUST VEGAN!

My dear fellow vegans, as The Vegan Society has chosen to use a noble cause to air his [*sic*] racialist thoughts, I will now leave this page. I think that we are not whites or blacks, we are humans, and it's as humans that we have to help the animals.

This is why racism is still so prevalent—because we continue to separate ourselves like this. Come on people.

Give us ONE example of black, white, green, yellow people being excluded from the vegan debate EVER since the world began, you numpties.

Why do we need black anything, how about just not mention race? Why do black people incessantly need their own everything?

This site should be about spreading word about animals and how it is morally unjust and wrong to abuse, profit, etc. off any animal, not about statistics about colour or race.

Why can't we just be vegans?

Why are we bringing race into this?

All vegans rock equally.

The discourse surrounding "All vegans rock" and "There are no white vegans, black vegans, red vegans . . . we are all vegans" is an extension of the "All Lives Matter" nonsense. Whenever black folks attempt to be specific about their own causes, we are called out for racism. Exclaiming "We are all vegans" is a way to employ post-racial rhetoric to violently silence activists of color who are trying to organize around their own experiences. Silencing vegans of color somehow translates to being "compassionate" for the animals. "All vegans rock" is a way to call activists of color "racist" for wanting to produce knowledge from their own standpoints, which is ironic given that the mainstream animal rights movement is structured through the experiences of the white dominant class.

These reactions are also troubling in an era where the word *intersectional* is often used to describe most of our social justice movements. It is possible to discuss more than one oppression at a time and it's OK to reexamine how these "isms" relate to one another. Conceptual violence creates the conditions for physical violence. The conceptual chains that oppress animals have been forged by race and gender constructs, which is why it's important to create theoretical tools to help break these chains. Setting animals free *physically* requires us to *conceptually* reevaluate all systems that have sustained and normalized their oppression.

4

By "Human," Everybody Just Means "White"

◆

Syl Ko
August 25, 2015

ANIMAL. WE, AS BLACK FOLKS, REACT VERY STRONGLY TO THIS WORD WHEN IT is used to draw any sort of relation or comparison to us. After all, the label *animal* was and continues to be one of the most destructive ever applied to us. One of the easiest ways to violate a person or group of people is to compare or reduce them to "animals." In March 2015, the San Francisco Police Department was investigated for racist and homophobic text exchanges. *Think Progress* reported on the story, stating, "The texts made public Friday included jokes about Kwanzaa, calling African Americans monkeys, calling for the lynching of all African Americans, and even one that said, 'Its [*sic*] not against the law to put an animal down.'"[1]

In her 1994 open letter to her colleagues, cultural theorist Sylvia Wynter noted, "You may have heard a radio news report which aired briefly during the days after the jury's acquittal of the policemen in the Rodney King beating case. The report stated that public officials of the judicial system of Los Angeles routinely used the acronym N.H.I. to refer to any case involving a breach of the rights of young Black males who belong to the jobless category of the inner city ghettos. N.H.I. means 'no humans involved.'"[2]

One could even argue that words like *nigger* or *thug* operate a lot like replacement terms for *animal*. Think about the ways that police (as well as everyday folks) justify violence toward black people by referring to them as "thugs" who need to be "controlled." It's no wonder that one way we have historically sought and continue to seek social visibility is by asserting our "humanity."

I used to be that kind of black activist. You know: *"We're human, too!"* But now, I question this strategy and want to investigate it in this chapter. How I see it is that the strategy of asserting one's humanity—humanization—is a lot like animalization.

With animalization, we are conceiving of a person or group as if they are animals. But with humanization, we're not acknowledging that one is a "human." We're conceiving a person or group *like* they are humans. So, my aim here is to persuade you that to demand that we be seen like we are human is racially loaded. If animalizing people is problematic, humanizing them is even worse, or so I suggest.

Since the terms *human* and *animal* are up for debate here, I will refer to what we ordinarily call humans as "homo sapiens" and what we ordinarily call animals as members of species "other than homo sapiens."

Of course, one major assumption behind both animalization and humanization is that those who are not members of homo sapiens just don't belong in the domain of moral or political consideration. I won't treat this issue directly but needless to say I think it's a view fraught with major problems.

Another assumption at work in these processes is that being "like an animal" is supposed to strike us as immediately intelligible. But the term *animal* refers to a fairly broad concept. There is no such thing as the general "animal," and I can't think of one feature or unifying behavior common only to all members of species other than homo sapiens. The only thing they have in common is they are not members of our species.

And what is "being human" like? At least here we have only one species to consider—*ours*. Maybe what it is like to "be human" is the wrong question to ask. After all, isn't being human just belonging to our species? So, why should humanization be a problem?

But *is* belonging to our species *really* what it is to "be human"? I don't think so. I think most people would distinguish "animal" from "human" behavior by appealing to something like "reason," "morality," our transcendence of the laws of nature, or something similar.

Or perhaps some of us might even say that human behavior is not to act "like an animal." For instance, the following passage from Douglas MacLean's article in *Philosophy & Public Policy Quarterly* (a reputable philosophy journal) would probably not be very controversial to most of us:

> Just as we have naming ceremonies for newborns, involve food in our rituals, go in for weddings, and do not disturb or desecrate graves, so it is part of what it means to be a human being that we don't eat off of the ground, defecate in public, or in other ways "behave like animals." It is only when we separate ourselves from nature in these ways that we make it possible to gain a sense of dignity, become suitable objects of respect, and make sense of moral behavior that is anything other than a set of instrumental relationships.[3]

Let's be honest about a few things. First, whether or not certain behaviors are ways in which we "behave like animals" is a somewhat subjective judgment. Secondly, the prioritizing of our "rational capacities" or the belief that engaging in certain practices "separates" us or puts us "above" nature are notions held by and tendencies in which only *certain* groups of people participate. And thirdly, those who prioritized our rational capacities and believed that their practices made them break with "nature" just happened to be those who decided which behaviors are reminiscent of "animals" and which weren't.

In fact, these people possess the most privilege in the world, thereby giving them the power not only to define the terms at play (*reason, nature,* and the terms in question—*human, animal*) but also to self-designate their group as behaving and looking distinctly *human*.

The domain of the "human" or "humanity" is not just about whether or not one belongs to the species homo sapiens. Rather, "human" means a certain way of being, especially exemplified by how one looks or behaves, what practices are associated with one's community, and so on. So, the "human" or what "humanity" is just is a *conceptual way to mark the province of European whiteness as the ideal way of being homo sapiens.*

This means that the conceptions of "humanity/human" and "animality/animal" have been constructed along *racial* lines. What is now understood to be *biological* was really European whites' self-conception and what they believed followed about the rest of the natural world in order to make this self-conception a *truth*.

Now, before I move on, I want to consider the following. Some of you might be thinking: members of homo sapiens divided themselves from all other species long before race entered the scene. At minimum, this divide was necessary so that other species could be used for food, clothing, labor, and a variety of other purposes. To see ourselves (homo sapiens) as different from all other species, however slight the *difference*, made it possible for us to exploit the latter, especially as food, and this played a major role in our evolutionary development from a physiological perspective. But it also played a major role in our development from a *cultural* perspective, given that many of our rituals and practices incorporate the use of animals in some way.

I certainly don't dispute this fact, although the ways in which this distinction was drawn and the degree to which there was ever a *clear* distinction probably varied among different groups of people. But let's bracket that information for the sake of getting to the point. I think it's a mistake to assume that the *modern* use of and subsequent attitude toward other species is a mere continuation of this homo sapiens "tradition." The introduction of race as a way of understanding geocultural, social, and individual identities completely changed our conceptual landscape. It continues to impact, in a deep sense, how we understand ourselves, each other, and the world.

With the invention of race came the reinvention of "man" or the "human." As the decolonial scholar Walter Mignolo describes it, "During the European renaissance, man [*sic*] was conceived at the intersection of his body and his mind, his body proportion and his intellect. Leonardo da Vinci's Vitruvian Man translated into visual language what humanists were portraying in words." As a result, "when the idea and the category of man came into the picture, it came already with a privilege" (p. 10).[4]

How so? Well, since European whites introduced the social construct of race for *their benefit*, they designated *themselves* and their point of reference as constitutive of "being human." They had the power to *universalize* whiteness as human. So, this new language of race posited the "human" in terms of naturalized whiteness.

What do I mean when I say that racial logic changed our conceptual landscape? Looking to gender as an example might help make sense of this claim. Feminist philosopher María Lugones notes that the norms of what it is to be a man or a woman were "premised upon the experiences of middle-class men and women of European origin."[5] She notes just how profoundly and cataclysmically this notion impacted non-European populations in the form of colonialism. Lugones draws on feminist scholar Oyèrónké Oyěwùmí's book *The Invention of Women*,[6] in which Oyěwùmí argues that prior to colonization the Yoruba society of present-day Nigeria did not have a gender system in place. Although they had terms to designate anatomic male and female, these categories were not understood to be hierarchical or binarily opposed.

Colonialism foisted onto different societies Eurocentric-constructed gender norms such that, for instance, what it was to be a woman involved a certain degree of whiteness, whether that be manifested in the shade of one's skin, the proportions of one's body, the hair's texture/length/style, the tone of voice, gait, and so on. Even to this day, conceptions of femininity and the ideal woman coincide with representations of whiteness.

Similarly, what it means to be "human" also underwent a drastic change after the introduction of racial logic, such that the term represented a particular population that had a certain way of being homo sapiens. But if this conception underwent such a drastic change after the introduction of race, it stands to reason that lots of other conceptions, especially those deeply connected to "human," were either distorted, reinvented, or generated under this new logic. Even relations were reinterpreted.

Lugones quotes sociologist Anibal Quijano: "The invention of race is a pivotal turn as it replaces the relations of superiority and inferiority established through domination. It reconceives humanity and human relations fictionally, in biological terms." This statement has interesting implications for how racial logic might affect our understanding of "animality/animal" and "humanity/human."[7] What is really the domination of one group by another is naturalized in terms of biological kinds.

With this in mind, we can go back to a question I raised earlier regarding what we mean when we hear something described as "animalistic" or "like an animal."

I noted that these types of descriptions involve an assumption that they are intelligible despite the fact that I really can't think of any obvious feature or behavior in which only members of species other than homo sapiens participate or that they possess. That is, how do these descriptions make sense when there just is no such thing as "*the* animal"? I think it is here wherein the *racial* construction of "the animal" can really be seen.

Although individual animal species may not in themselves be construed in terms of race, the conception of "the animal" or "the general animal" operates in conjunction with its racial analog, "the human" or "the general human." If "the human" is really an expression of whiteness as the ideal way of being homo sapiens, then "the animal" is supposed to express a *deviation* from this way of being. "The general animal," then, applies not only to members of other species, who clearly cannot participate in such a form of life by virtue of not having even the necessary features to "be human," but it can also apply to those members of homo sapiens who deviate from the way whites look and/or behave, and what values and commitments they hold, and so forth.

On this interpretation, humanization is not merely the act of asserting that one is homo sapiens. That would be futile. Rather, humanization is the act of asserting one's resemblance to "humans"—white people.

When we refer to a person or a group as "animalistic," we are not really saying they bear some generic strong resemblance to species other than homo sapiens. This would make no sense because, again, there is no such thing as a generic non–homo sapiens property. What we are saying is *they don't behave or look or believe properly*, where what is "proper" is defined by Eurocentric, white ideals. In other words, they *deviate from whiteness*.

"Appropriate" ways of looking and carrying oneself are standard-ized by whites; "respectable" religions and "proper" rituals of belief are standardized by whites; the most "useful" ways of thinking about and engaging with the world are standardized by whites, and so on. Anything that doesn't have an air of white familiarity to it is "exotic," "primitive," "irrational," "animalistic." You get the picture.

So, now what? Obviously, I strongly support moving away from the strategy of humanization, at least in the way it currently stands. First of all, from a practical viewpoint, it just won't work. If humanity is defined in terms of whiteness, then at best most of us will be living in the shadow of what Western whites deem is the way to live, look, behave, believe, know, celebrate, and so on. More importantly, when we attempt to "humanize" ourselves, and when we glamorize "the human," we uphold the superiority of whiteness.

Having said that, I also don't think the way to move forward is to try to disentangle whiteness from our conception of "human." For instance, some might think it would be a good idea to reconceive (*really* reconceive) humanity in terms of species. Namely, any member of homo sapiens qual-ifies as human regardless of one's features or practices or history. But this way of thinking seems to overlook completely the fact that "human" and "animal," especially understood in relation to one another, *are deeply embedded in the grammar of racial logic*. If we want to free ourselves and others who have suffered from the racialization of the world, why play along with the game of defining "human"? Why not move away from this imperial project altogether and recast the terms of liberation, for ourselves and for others, in a completely new language and vision of the world?

I acknowledge that I'm painting an incomplete picture here. But I wanted to express these thoughts in order to inspire some reflection. In closing, I'd like to leave you with a few conclusions that follow from the thoughts presented here.

First, I think we as black people seriously need to reconsider our relationship with nonhuman animals. When we make use of the human–animal binary to justify our attitudes toward other species, we are in fact using the very same racial logic that posits the "human" as whiteness. There is already a movement underway in which people from our community call upon members to "decolonize" our bodies, our diets, and areas of activism. But we also need to decolonize the frameworks that govern our concepts. For those of us in the West who can afford to live otherwise, our comfort with using animals, especially as meat and dairy, only reveals our comfort with white-centric modes of thinking. Dismantling racism might require dismantling our patterns of consumption, including our food practices.

Secondly and closely related, I think those of us who *do* see a need to address the situation of nonhuman animals need to steer clear of the mainstream tendency to simplify issues having to do with animality in terms of speciesism alone. Right now, a lot of tension exists in mainstream animal rights spaces, with many questioning the relevance of racial issues beyond their use in drawing up productive analogies. Understanding the "human" and "animal" in this more nuanced sense should spark a commitment in our community to understand the white/black and human–animal binaries as not merely bearing upon one another but *deeply intertwined*, with all four terms functioning to uphold the superiority of whiteness.

Author's note: Please see chapter 17 ("Revaluing the Human as a Way to Revalue the Animal") for a follow-up to this discussion.

5

Why Confusion Is Necessary for Our Activism to Evolve

◆

Aph Ko
September 2, 2015

Have you ever encountered someone who eats meat and bombards you with thousands of scenario-based questions when you confront them over his or her eating patterns? This person usually says, "Well, what would we do with all of the animals in factory farms if factory farms ended? Would you just release them all at once? Wouldn't that be a problem?" Or, have you ever been in conversation with someone about ending the prison system and the person says, "Well, if we end prisons, what are we supposed to do with all of the prisoners? Just let them out?" Though these questions are frustrating and at times predictable, they demonstrate how people are colonized by the mainstream system to the extent they can't even imagine new possibilities for themselves. They can't imagine a different setup from the one that's been imposed on them.

Part of activism is finding yourself in a new space of confusion, allowing yourself to step into new conceptual terrain. When you abandon commonly held oppressive beliefs, you might not exactly know what to do afterward, and that's where more activists *need* to be. Confusion is usually a symptom of decolonizing yourself from the mainstream system. Answers aren't easily laid out in front of you since you're now forced to think critically. You have to create new blueprints and imagine new ways of interacting with people and doing things. Often, people who are colonized by the contemporary system ask questions in a patronizing way because they don't want change to happen, because most people thrive on comfort. Change is a threat.

I remember I once told a sexist professor at my university that I was a feminist. We had a meeting that finished and we were heading out of the building. As we were walking to the exit, he asked me, "Well, I know you're a feminist and I don't want to offend you or anything, but can I open the door for you? Do you allow men to open your doors or are you going to be offended?"

Of course, he was asking me this in a patronizing way to mock my political beliefs. However, his questions made me realize how *he* was the one with the anxiety because he didn't want to confront his own confusion surrounding gendered interactions. It was *he* who was anxious about what to do when it came to opening the door, not me. In fact, I'm certain that as women gained more rights in the US, men who were conditioned to think we were silly playthings reacted by negatively pointing out how confused *they* were now. *Do I pay for the meal? Do I buy flowers? Do I open the door?*

I would argue that confusion is a *good* thing.

The resurgence in such talk, wherein people keep asking if "chivalry is dead" or if it should come back, isn't coincidental; it's a backlash at feminist advances. My generation of so-called millennials has a particular nostalgia for gallantry because it was evidently "so much easier back then"—to live during a time when such behaviors were advertised because you didn't have to question them: society told you what to do, how to dress, how to behave, and you were rewarded for following the scripts.

Many chauvinistic men who cling to gender norms of the past blame feminism for contributing to their confusion when they encounter women today. They assume that gendered interactions are much more stressful than before. However, being confused about how to talk and be with women is valuable. It means you no longer view all women through a single lens, where we're all easily impressed with faux attempts at respect (opening the door, but not taking my voice seriously). Confusion means you've stepped into new terrain and you actually have to *think*. Not knowing what to do because your culture is changing is catalytic. It offers moments when your colonized self is confronting or colliding with your "decolonizing" self.

The only way we can build from the ground up is to allow ourselves to be confused. Our activist spaces are in turmoil precisely because people don't want to accommodate this necessary confusion. *Intersectionality* may be a fun word to toss around, but people are scared to make connections in their movements because they will have to create new blueprints for their activism. This is difficult, especially if your particular style of activism has become an identity for you.

So many of the ways we conduct our activism operate on scripts and mantras but don't foster critical thinking or questioning. In fact, I'm finding that areas where we engage with others in activism can be quite violent, because they often reproduce the very problems they're fighting against. Even social justice movements that dogmatically cling to intersectionality are relatively uncritical spaces in which people are looking for a framework to *follow*, not a framework to critically *think* through. When you engage in critical thinking, you don't necessarily cling to a model or one specific way of viewing the world; you are always shifting and changing perspectives.

As I wrote in chapter 3, white vegans attacked my 100 Black Vegans article because they felt that focusing on race and animality within the context of animal rights would distract from helping "the animals." Although many people were angry, some actually seemed *afraid* that their movement was changing—even to the extent of claiming that people who talk about race and animality (like me) are in a "cult." (I'm not kidding.) No, I'm not in a cult. In fact, if you can't interpret my actions or theory as anything other than cultlike, then maybe *you* are actually a member of a group with a fixed view of the world.

Because there's an already-established blueprint for engaging in animal rights work and activism, some folks get afraid when they see it being done differently. When they notice that some activists are attempting to show how speciesism connects with racism and sexism, they grow fearful because it's not "usually" done like that. I see a similar anxiety in main-stream anti-racist movements. When I bring up animality and race, I'm usually confronted with *immediate* resistance from black folks who don't think speciesism has anything to do with racism. In fact, I tend to face humiliation in multiple online and physical locations that already have a specific way of conducting anti-racist activist work, because the frame-works they employ are not designed to interpret theory that politicizes animality and white supremacy.

I understand intimately how daunting it can be when you are exposed to a theory that turns your activism on its head. Recently, when I was preparing for a presentation, I'd *almost* completed my notes when I *happened* to read a few articles from Tommy Curry, an Africana philosopher, that challenge the ways in which people talk and theorize about black men and racial violence.[1] Dr. Curry posits that black men don't just experience *racism*, they simultaneously experience *sexual racism* considering that they are routinely harassed sexually and raped by police officers[2] (which the mainstream news media tend to exclude in their analyses of racism and police violence), and have undergone sexual trauma dating back to slavery.

Dr. Curry brilliantly points out that when we frame gender-based violence as solely a phenomenon that revolves around women (particu-larly white women), we erase the ways that white women have histori-cally assaulted black men and continue to commit sexual violence on black men's bodies.[3] These articles *shattered* the intersectional frameworks I had been using in my activism, and I remember panicking because I *agreed* with the author, and in agreeing with him I assumed my whole presentation was invalid because I saw so many gaps in my own theories and thoughts. However, I integrated his theories into my presentation because I was eager to introduce these provocative and life-changing ideas to my audience.

Unfortunately, a lot of activists don't allow their cherished theories and practices to be altered in such a manner. Some would much rather stay in an oppressive system as long as they have some semblance of power and control, rather than engage with new ideas that incorporate new voices, because they destabilize their feelings of control.

In March 2015, I attended a lecture by Angela Davis at a women's studies conference. The section of her dazzling talk that resonated with me most was her analysis of how activists often reproduce oppressive behaviors by not allowing themselves to change their viewpoints. In essence, she stated that we all use frameworks for our activism. When someone offers us new information that *should* disrupt our framework, many of us cling even harder to our viewpoints and frameworks because we're scared to change. There is seemingly nothing worse for an activist than being introduced to a new perspective or theory that challenges the way you've been doing things. Rather than acting as though that perspective doesn't exist, Professor Davis suggested we should immerse ourselves in it and allow ourselves to be confronted. Our reflex to turn the other way as activists is a product of being colonized.

We need to encourage people to question their behaviors so they're in a conceptual terrain of confusion, which is one of the most revolutionary areas to be in because we're not bound by oppressive behaviors and norms. In this space, we all have the power to be conceptual architects. Questions dismantle cultural scripts and confusion can produce new blueprints for change. Confusion is a necessary phase in activism, and if you find that you're rarely confused and rarely challenged, then you might be operating from a script yourself.

6

WOMEN, BEAUTY, AND NATURE

◆

Syl Ko
September 11, 2015

A DISTANT ACQUAINTANCE OF MINE RECENTLY RETURNED FROM A TRIP abroad during which he was exposed to what he described as a "peculiar" tendency present in the way many local, indigenous people in the region talked about nature. He said something like, "I swear, it's like these people have absolutely no appreciation for nature. They are surrounded by some of the most beautiful landscapes I have ever seen and when I mentioned it, they looked at me like they were bored." When a friend said that perhaps they weren't particularly moved by the scenery because they were just used to it, the distant acquaintance said, "Honestly, you could probably drop these people in front of Mount Everest for the first time and I'd imagine they wouldn't give a shit."

In the midst of his culturally insensitive rambling, my acquaintance stumbled onto something rather interesting. He noted that, although to him those of us in the "West" seem to be better able to "grasp" how beautiful nature is, that doesn't seem to stop us from ruining it. The same people in favor of tearing down trees for a new building or wider streets, or complicit in consumption patterns they know will negatively impact the environment, also travel far and wide to personally witness, climb, and extensively photograph gorgeous mountains, or trek through lush rainforests or dip into impossibly blue natural pools of water. As they travel, they are insistent: *Isn't it all so beautiful? Can you believe it?* And when they return, they are struck by a newfound connection with nature because they spent some time "there," in the middle of it all, feeling its majesty and their own smallness, dazzled by its beauty.

In the same week as my acquaintance made his observation, an older graduate student gave a presentation on a section of his dissertation in which he also shared some experiences from a long trip to a few regions in South America. During that time, he also mostly engaged with local, indigenous people, with whom he has some family ties, for the purpose of trying to understand their ways of knowing, which differed quite significantly from the typical Western ones.

I won't go into the details of the indigenous people's views, but one general, interesting fact the student presented was that there was no concept of "nature" in their language. That is, there was no sense in which we—human beings—were over *here* as perceiving subjects or knowers, whereas "nature" was over *there*, a passive object to be experienced and known. Rather, the people he encountered saw themselves in a deep relationship with the surrounding plants, animals, bodies of water, and so on, such that there was no distance that enabled any being to be only and permanently an object. This got me thinking about my culturally insensitive acquaintance's comments. He interpreted the people's reaction to "nature" as them not appreciating its beauty. Our mutual friend assumed instead that perhaps they were just used to it since they lived there and saw it every day. Who knows, maybe he's right?

I have a third interpretation, in light of this new information about some peoples' very different, non-Eurocentric conceptual resources. Since they did not put any distance between themselves and the other citizens of "nature," since nonhuman entities were not strange, alien, passive objects to be witnessed or understood from "over here," but instead deeply connected, continuous beings who themselves could be co-subjects with the people, this particular people considered the stuff that we call "nature" *simply not the right kinds of beings/things to be thought of as essentially objects of beauty.*

In a way, some feminists have similar thoughts about the mainstream's obsession with women and beauty. For several years, films and TV shows, magazines, fashion shows, or commercials have been congratulating themselves for featuring "real" women. Instead of endorsing the ridiculously narrow standard of beauty (tall, thin, doll-faced, usually white, hyperfeminine, and sexualized), these "progressive" campaigns champion "real" women, hoping to widen the range of the beauty standard to include *all* women. Basically, the notion can be summed up as "all women are beautiful!"

Although some feminists are fighting to ensure all women (and not just white, thin ones), are beautiful, others—like myself—are critical of the connection between beauty and women altogether. We ask the question: *Why do women have to be thought of as beautiful?* That women are automatically connected with beauty is problematic in a number of ways, but I'll only discuss the way it is relevant to the discussion I raised above regarding nature.

I think one major reason women are *essentially* tied to beauty, to being observed and physically admired, is because they have traditionally been cast as *distinct* from men, so distinct that it is not uncommon to hear about men who are *afraid* of women. Most of us are probably familiar with the following scenes either from TV, the movies, or real life: a woman enters the comic book store or game convention only to have the men tremble in fear and run away; a woman joins a predominantly male workplace or classroom or team and whereas some of the men make creepy advances to her, others are "afraid" to strike up a conversation with her or they go out of their way to avoid her because they "don't know how to talk to women."

The obsession with women being *different*, special, alien, *remote*, so hard to understand and "figure out," and so on is premised on the distance culturally placed between the sexes. The artificial distance between us almost nullifies the fact that women *themselves* are subjects.

Since the male viewpoint is commonly centered and objective, women are seen as the deviation from the norm; *they* are the ones who are scary, strange, and *beautiful*. They are to be grasped "from afar," passive objects to be understood and figured out, and physically observed and admired. Women have a perpetual object status and are tied to beauty in a way that men cannot be.

Of course, this isn't to say that men cannot be appreciated for how they look or there is something problematic about finding women beautiful. That's not the point. The problem is that "all women are beautiful!" is not only comprehensible to us but also seen as *progressive*. I'm beautiful when I wake up in the morning, when I'm in the middle of a grueling six-mile run, and when I'm not particularly interested or invested in being beautiful.

Why am I beautiful? *Because I'm a woman.* I am *always* the right kind of being to admire in that particular way. I'm perpetually an object. It is a *part of my nature* to be an object of beauty, to be admired.

The very same thing that affords us this status of perpetual beauty, however, also makes us *exploitable*. Because we are distanced from subject-hood, because we are alien and *different*, mystical creatures, passive beautiful things to be apprehended from afar, we are also forced into perpetual object status.

I think something similar is going on with the nature-as-beautiful rhetoric. If we were to regard "nature" in such a way that we were so deeply related to it that the concept wouldn't even make sense to us, perhaps it would be strange to think of it primarily in terms of aesthetics. There just isn't enough distance to get the fixed subject/object distinction off the ground to make "nature" a perpetual object of beauty or for those types of judgments even to be noteworthy. If there is no such distance, then certainly "nature" would not be seen as exploitable. After all, the deep relations to it would prevent us from being able even to *conceive* of it as something "out there," something deeply different, an object and a resource. Rather, we would operate in conjunction, as co-subjects, as continuous.

7

Emphasizing Similarities Does Nothing for the Oppressed

◆

Syl Ko
September 29, 2015

AROUND A YEAR AGO, PROFESSOR ROBERT SUSSMAN, AUTHOR OF *THE MYTH OF Race: The Troublesome Persistence of an Unscientific Idea*, raised a question in *Newsweek*: "Unfortunately, along with the belief in the reality of biologically based human races, racism still abounds in the United States and Western Europe. How can this be when there is so much scientific evidence against it?"[1] In his article, Sussman presents a list, which includes a diversity of attributes, capacities, dispositions, and the like, which many Americans continue to associate with racial differences.

For instance, many people still believe that race (*independent of* social and other forces) heavily factors into intelligence, work ethic/abilities, sexual behavior, infant care, personal restraint, aggression, altruism, and family cohesion. Sussman claims: "We humans are more similar to each other as a group than we are to one another within any particular racial or genetic category." Therefore, despite the wealth of data that reveal the overwhelming *similarities* between members of different races, thereby suggesting that racial differences don't really amount to much more than just skin color (independent of social forces), people continue to hold certain attitudes and exhibit certain behaviors that would suggest otherwise.[2]

A similar phenomenon exists with our attitudes and beliefs toward most animals. Historically, humans and animals were thought to be discontinuous entities: humans had souls whereas animals were soulless, and thus couldn't be "saved" . . . though they could be possessed by the devil, apparently, not to mention tried in court;[3] humans had minds whereas animals were mere machinelike automatons,[4] and so on. Nowadays, it is more or less accepted that variations among species are best understood as differences in degree, not kind.

Moreover, despite differences in degree, many different species *share* in activities, behaviors, and capacities initially thought to be exclusively the province of homo sapiens. Philosopher Cary Wolfe notes: "[PBS] and cable television—most recently in the big budget PBS series on 'the animal mind' hosted by *Nature* executive producer George Page—have made standard fare out of one study after another convincingly demonstrating that the traditionally distinctive marks of the human (first it was possession of a soul, then 'reason,' then tool use, then tool making, then altruism, then language, then the production of linguistic novelty, and so on) flourish quite reliably beyond the species barrier."[5]

Similarly, evolutionary biologist Marc Bekoff, who cofounded Ethologists for the Ethical Treatment of Animals with Jane Goodall, remarked in an article for *Psychology Today*, "Animal Minds and the Foible of Human Exceptionalism": "The database grows daily and science is supporting many of our intuitions about the cognitive, emotional, and moral capacities for complex forms of consciousness."[6] Bekoff goes on to say, "We're clearly neither the only conscious beings nor the sole occupants of the emotional and moral arenas in which there are also some surprising residents including honeybees, fish, and chickens. Surely we have no right to intrude wantonly into the lives of other animals or to judge them or blame them for our evil ways."

A trove of data exists that, in the case of racism, dispels the myth that people of color are somehow deeply or *essentially* distinct from white people. In the case of what is commonly referred to as speciesism, the data dispel the myth that animals are irredeemably foreign or dissimilar to us in their capacities, activities, and interests. Despite this, racism and speciesism remain fully entrenched in our society.[7]

There is an obvious *activist* component to many of these studies, searching for and revealing meaningful similarities among presumably "different" beings.[8] That is, those of us who wish to ensure visibility, protection, and justice for marginalized, oppressed, and/or exploited groups assume that pointing to and proving robust similarities between the oppressed group in question and the dominant group will give the dominant group less reason to continue harming members of the oppressed group, or be less comfortably complicit with harms.

As a result, drawing connections between the behaviors, characteristics, interests, and capacities of marginalized and dominant beings is supposed to offer reliable grounds for enhancing marginalized beings' rights or calling for justice in enforcing them. As Wolfe puts it with respect to animals, "In the light of developments in cognitive science, ethology, and other fields over the past twenty years . . . it seems clear that there is no longer any good reason to take it for granted that the theoretical, ethical, and political question of the subject is automatically coterminous with the species distinction between Homo Sapiens and everything else."

There are many things to be said here. For instance, most studies require rigorous interpretive work, which may lead to conclusions that are hard to accept, especially concerning animals. I'm going to overlook the interpretive issue and grant that, for the sake of simplicity, the studies do in fact present compelling reasons for thinking a substantial overlap exists between human and animal capacities, social behaviors, interests, and so forth. (That differences between groups of beings result in judgments about relative inferiority and superiority is a research project of its own.)

What I am mostly concerned with here is the following assumption: that if we—a privileged group—neglect certain beings, or fail to extend to them rights or other sorts of protections, or if we systematically harm those beings, then it must have something to do with the fact that they are "not like us" in relevant ways.

In other words, I believe that *the popular move to stress marginalized and privileged groups' similarities and to minimize their differences is motivated by the implicit assumption that these presumed differences are fueling the disparity in treatment.* So, by proving a meaningful continuity between these groups or proving they are significantly alike in ways that are important to the privileged group, we thereby lose reasons for differential allocation of resources or protections, and so on, and effect a change in treatment owed to the marginalized group in question.

For instance, one of the most common responses to careless, racist claims is to appeal to scientific studies (natural and/or social) in order to assert that, fundamentally, "we are all the same." Another popular way to respond to racist claims might involve acknowledging the wide disparities between IQ levels, income, incarceration rates, and so on among different racial groups but to stress that all of these would be relatively equivalent had the economic, political, and historical context for certain people of color been different.[9] Or consider the work of Cheikh Anta Diop, physicist, historian, and anthropologist, who, among other things, set out to show that precolonial Africans had similar intellectual and artistic values and standards as Western Europeans and shared in the legacy of forming great civilizations and producing great works of art, science, and the like.[10]

Now, I certainly think there is great value in some studies that show we've been exaggerating differences between groups or that we have been ignoring significant similarities. I also believe that, fundamentally, we *are* "all the same," and I agree that, had the economic, political, social, and historical contexts been different, the various disparities we observe between racial groups would be less pronounced, if present at all. Also, I don't dispute the results that follow from Diop's research.

I also think it's worth mentioning that *of course* there were and continue to be projects deeply invested in emphasizing or inventing distinctions among groups *precisely for the purpose of* perpetuating exploitation and oppression.

What I take issue with is the assumption that phenomena like racism or speciesism (not to mention other pernicious "isms") are caused by or can be explained by appealing to data (real or imagined) about differences in capacities, intelligence, behaviors, features, and so on. Certainly, given the amount of effort spent creating or stressing differences among groups, this type of information (again, real or fabricated) plays a role in helping to *maintain* and especially to *make normal* specific oppressions and exploitation. But this information is not where the phenomena of racism, speciesism, and other "isms" bottom out.

Philosopher Cora Diamond, who is deeply invested in the animal situation, distinguishes differences between humans and animals and *the difference* (her term) between humans and animals. Although the sciences can speak to the former, the latter, she writes, is established by "an idea that we form, a concept we create knowing full well the obvious similarities between us. . . . It's not a difference we discover because of ethology or evolutionary history." Thus, whereas learning more about the bodies, minds, and social environments of animals might minimize the differences between humans and animals, it doesn't follow that *the difference* is also diffused.

In other words, *the difference* between humans and animals, the crucial factor that fuels the phenomenon of speciesism, was not born from the observation that animals are irredeemably foreign or dissimilar to us. In fact, Diamond points to the contrary ("[*the difference*] is a concept we create knowing full well the obvious similarities between us").

These claims, which come from Diamond's invaluable 1978 paper "Eating Meat and Eating People,"[11] are central to her view that typical intellectual animal rights arguments are neither effective (on the large scale) nor do they get to the heart of *why* animal exploitation, torture, and slaughter happen. The "difference" is, in the case of humans and animals, *created by us* as a functional device. As a result, many terms that are animal-specific *carry within them* the parameters for how to treat that being. Appealing to anything external, such as their capacity to suffer, misses the force of concepts and *how* they function.

For example, just calling someone an "animal" or "nonhuman" is more than enough to justify extreme violence toward that person. The justification is *in the choice of that term itself.* There is no need to appeal to anything external. Or, as Diamond points out, calling someone a "person" denotes that it is not the kind of thing to be eaten. By simply *choosing* the term *person* as the *right* term for a certain being, you thereby grasp that you cannot eat him or her.

I think something similar occurs with racial terms. Frantz Fanon argued in his groundbreaking book *Black Skin, White Masks* that racializing beings actually *constructs* bodies and psyches. It's not the case that the presumed inferiority of the African was observed or located in the *actual* body. Rather, the inferiority is locked into and is part and parcel of the racial *label* of *Negro* or *black,* and the system that gave rise to the label. The "black" or "Negro" is the location and source of the African's inferiority, where the "blackness" is *fictive*—a creation by Western Europeans.

Since the site of *the difference* between "whites" and "blacks" does not reside in *actual* differences between the groups, all of the data in the world will not do anything to dissolve racism. Natural and social scientific data draw on actual, real bodies, behaviors, capacities, interests, and such.[12] Racism, however, draws on the *created,* raced body. So, although it might help the racist cause to stress differences between groups, emphasizing similarities won't do much to alleviate racism.

A more effective way to address these phenomena, which stem from a fictional difference (Diamond's *the difference*) is to reveal, first, the source of the fiction and then, secondly, uproot the source by changing the terms of the conversation.[13] If white supremacy, which authored the racial classification system during its colonial infancy, is the source, how do we dismantle it?

I propose we change the terms of the conversation by *refusing to center whiteness* in our lives and work. I have explored this topic already; however, in short, de-centering whiteness essentially means we need to take seriously non-white theoretical constructs and frameworks and use these to change our understanding of the world, others, and ourselves. These theoretical models *take white supremacy and white superiority as starting points,* as a reality, and as *the* fundamental threat to justice everywhere. I also think de-centering whiteness requires taking seriously non-white art, literature, music, systems of belief, and other rituals as a way of reimagining the world outside of the constraints developed by white supremacy.

As I've already argued, I think refusing to center whiteness also encourages us to move away from the human–animal divide.[14] (Since I've already explored this topic at length, I invite you to read through the cited post at your convenience.)

Of course, the title to this chapter—"Emphasizing Similarities Does Nothing for the Oppressed"—might be too forceful for some. Ultimately, it's an empirical matter whether or not this or that strategy works. I don't necessarily think there's *one* strategy that is *the* strategy for effectively addressing matters such as racism or speciesism. I hope drawing attention to the *conceptual* and *invented* roots of these phenomena will spark more commitment to actively de-link ourselves from Eurocentric, white-supremacist ways of thinking.

8

Addressing Racism Requires Addressing the Situation of Animals

◆

Syl Ko
October 26, 2015

How we choose to address and "do something" about the violation or harms committed against vulnerable groups matter. Understandably, we want to *feel* like we *are* "doing something" about a problem and, in wanting to feel that way, we rush to "do" that "something." But many times, by rushing to "do something" about a problem, we unintentionally reproduce or perpetuate the violence or harm against which we protest, precisely through the methods or ways of thinking we employ.

Sometimes it doesn't occur to us that the unglamorous work of thinking about and discussing *how* we should do something about some problem *is* doing something about the problem. It's only by discussing and thinking about how that problem arises, how it presents itself, how it's maintained, that we start to locate what the problem *is*. And often-times, the problem looks starkly different from when those discussions first began.

The ideological foundation for the website Aphro-ism is the result of years of discussions between Aph and myself surrounding issues having to do with being black women in the United States. Eventually, those discussions began to extend to how our struggle is related to the struggles of other racialized groups in the US and to the struggles of racialized groups across the globe. We were encouraged to create this unique space after realizing that we have a very different way of understanding what the problem *is* for racialized folks and, thus, for how we ought to proceed in our activism given this rearticulation of the problem.

We think that something crucial has been missing from most discussions about racism and from *almost all strategies* to resist or combat racism: the situation of animals.

Now of course, people of color in activist spaces touch upon "the animal," at least conceptually, in some way. For instance, almost any good analysis of racism or coloniality usually calls attention to the degree to which racialized folks are *animalized*. That is, we animalize or *dehumanize* certain folks, individually or as groups, thereby justifying their violation.[1]

Law professor Maneesha Deckha notes that, "infliction on animal bodies is perceived as legitimate violence because of the nonhuman status of the species involved."[2] As a result, if we can persuade the mainstream that certain groups fall outside of "human"—they are irrational, they hold "barbaric" values, they have "inferior" systems of beliefs, they behave "like animals," and so on—we legitimize acting against these groups in ways that would otherwise be considered grossly inappropriate and criminal.

Interestingly, however, most of the analysis in anti-racist discourse concerning animality stops there. What usually follows is protestation about the animalization of groups of color. People of color are humans, too; so, we should treat them as humans, not animals. Notice that there is an *open acceptance* of the negative status of "the animal" here which, as I see it, is a *tacit acceptance* of *the hierarchical racial system and white supremacy in general*.

The human–animal divide is the ideological bedrock underlying the framework of white supremacy. The negative notion of "the animal" is the *anchor* of this system.

"White" is not just the superior race; it is also the superior mode of *being*. Residing at the top of the racial hierarchy is the white *human*, where species and race *coincide* to create the master being. Resting at the bottom as the abject opposite of the human, of whiteness, is the (necessarily) nebulous notion of "the animal."[3]

Quoting from Sherene Razack's excellent 2007 book on the absence of Muslims from Western law titled *Casting Out: The Eviction of Muslims from Western Law and Politics*, Deckha states: "It is species-thinking that helps to create the racial demarcation. Race-thinking, the denial of a common bond of humanity between people of European descent and those who are not, is a defining feature of the world order today as in the past."[4]

The racial hierarchy and racism, not to mention the racial thinking it generates, was the novel way white, Western Europeans in the colonial period legally and morally placed groups outside the "human" zone. As a result, the authors of this system were deeply invested in a rigid species divide where "human" indicated the domain of morality and law, and "animal" was a space of absence of being and lawlessness, inviting a need to be controlled, disciplined, and contained by "humans."[5]

As authors of the racial framework, Western white men conceived of *themselves* as the representatives of humanity. *They* were the objects of morality and law and, not coincidentally, the subjects that *dictated how* we should think about notions such as morality, law, and justice.

Their notion of "the animal"—construed under their white supremacist framework as "subhuman," "nonhuman," or "inhuman"—is the *conceptual vehicle for justified violence* or, as Deckha also puts it, a "violence producing category." Since racism *requires* this notion of animality, since racism and race-thinking would fail to *make sense* without animality, those of us interested in resisting or combatting racism need to take seriously why the status of "the animal" is what it is.

When we excuse a harm committed against a being saying, "It's just an animal," we need to interrogate the "just" in use here. The human–animal divide (binary), where "the human" and "the animal" form oppositional poles and, thus, oppositional status-markers on a "chain of being," is not an objective model handed to us from the heavens. "The human" and "the animal" were placed through the *positing of a racial system*.[6] In the same vein, racial categories tracking modes of "being" and degrees of superiority/inferiority are not part of an objective framework that must be in place for us to think about or conceptually arrange members of the world. Both of these frameworks, which are *deeply intertwined, and cannot be made sense of independent of one another,* were *creations* invented by a small percentage of people who took themselves to be the singular point of knowledge and, through centuries of violence, genocide, and control made their view of the world, themselves, and others *universal.*[7]

It is clear to me that if we truly want to take white supremacy, racism, coloniality (however one wants to talk about it) to task, then we need to do the same to the continuing, uncontroversial view that "the animal" is the *opposite status-marker* to "the human."

As long as these notions of "the animal" and "the human" are intact, white supremacy remains intact.

For this reason, I have advised against the strategy of "humanizing" groups of color, or gaining protections for vulnerable groups on the basis of *their humanity.* Deckha similarly warns us about relying on theories in which the subhuman is crucial, such as humanist and liberal theories: "Whether motivated by a focus on human vulnerability, nonhuman vulnerability, or both, pursuing anti-violence projects with the current anthropocentric status quo seriously undercuts those very same projects."[8]

As a result of holding this unique position—namely, that uprooting white supremacy is going to involve uprooting the human–animal divide—we have to be creative about how to proceed in our activism. As just mentioned, we have to steer clear of theories that fundamentally rely on the human–animal divide. Although utilizing the human–animal divide might bring some relief to a situation, it does nothing to get at the *root* of the problem, the bedrock of white supremacist logic. By settling for temporary improvements without addressing the "violence producing category" of the animal/subhuman/nonhuman, we invite guaranteed future harms, which—given technological advancements—will be more destructive than ever before.

Since we think a serious commitment to anti-racism will involve a deep commitment to animals, the direct bearers of the unfortunate consequences of the negative status-marker "the animal," we also have to be careful with typical approaches to extending concern to animals.

Like the mainstream anti-racist initiatives, which fail to consider the *species* element of racist logic, many mainstream anti-speciesist initiatives fail to consider the very same thing present in speciesist logic. But, relatedly and more importantly, as I mentioned before, white Western men took it upon themselves to be the *sole voices* for how we should think about notions such as justice and morality, not to mention a host of other crucial ideas hidden in our ways of thinking about the world.

A big part of fighting racism is *rejecting the position that white, Western voices and views are the only legitimate voices and views in the world.*

I don't see why we have to try to *extend* the views of, say, John Rawls or Immanuel Kant instead of just turning to other views, rooted in different, anti-racist traditions, or even coming up with our own. I don't see why we have to honor the hyper-obsession with the "person" or the "individual" in the West and try to extend personhood or individuality to animals in order to rethink/reimagine animality. We could just resist this obsession altogether—resist the idea that concern, care, or protections are supposed to correlate with "an individual." I don't see why we have to try to find some abstract principle or some capacity or feature that is the "universal status-conferring" capacity or feature and try to prove that this applies to all of the beings we wish to cover.

But I also don't think the way to go about doing the uprooting work I've recommended is to avoid terminology that is key to this discussion: pretending the notions of "human" and "animal" do not exist or that they cannot be useful. This approach could be a disastrous, even dangerous, method to employ, and so I don't recommend it—for the same reason I don't encourage avoiding racial terms or pretending they don't exist. Avoidance is ineffective and does nothing to address racism or the situation of animals and, in fact, can help *maintain* these phenomena.

For instance, although US laws do not make any explicit reference to races anymore, they are just as effective in maintaining racism. Avoiding these key terms as an uprooting strategy is to misunderstand the nature of words and notions, and how deeply entrenched they are in our attitudes, practices, and institutions, whether or not we explicitly refer to them.

I've tried to make the case that anti-racist work will require a liberation that we may not have initially expected: liberation from the human–animal divide, and, as a result, severing the connection between "animality" and "non-status." I'll also say that, given my view, I'm taking the position that the best case in favor of defending animals from violation is going to be generated from *within the anti-racist commitment*. Unlike others, I don't see these as competing commitments and, in fact, I think these issues must be addressed together.

9

WHY BLACK VEGANISM IS MORE THAN JUST BEING BLACK AND VEGAN

◆

Syl Ko and Aph Ko
November 11, 2015

ONE OF THE MOST FREQUENT QUESTIONS WE ENCOUNTER IS: *WHAT DOES RACE have to do with veganism? Veganism is supposed to be all about the animals!*

Now, this question (and general sentiment) has been posed to us in a variety of contexts, and so, depending on the context, the way one might go about addressing it changes. But in this chapter we want to focus specifically on perhaps the most popular phenomenon that invites this question, which is the tendency for some people to *mark or highlight their racial or ethnic identity* when aligning themselves with an ideology, movement, lifestyle, or activism.

Of course, this tendency is not peculiar to vegan/animal advocacy spaces; nor is it peculiar to only people of color. There exist black, Indigenous, Latina, and other types of feminisms. Or queer Marxist sites of activism, and so on. But this tendency seems different given in those cases it's clear that people are gesturing to *plural* identities they share, and it makes quite a difference when addressing sexism or classism whether or not we are discussing *racialized* or *marginalized* subjects confronting these issues.

Even if people understand why, say, feminisms must be marked by the identities of its participants, it might not be so easy to understand why veganism should be marked in this way. After all, veganism just seems different because of the centrality of the nonhuman victims we are supposed to be addressing. This is not about *us*; it's about *them*. Leaving aside the problematic history of terms like *human* and *animal*, *we* are not supposed to be the focus of veganism—*animals are*.

So, what's going on here? And doesn't this tendency to mark or highlight our racial/ethnic identities in vegan spaces pollute or interfere with the message of veganism? Again, what does race have to do with veganism?

1. Black Vegans

To begin with, race need not have anything to do with veganism in the deep sense, depending on one's understanding of the animal situation. We know plenty of black vegans who couldn't care less about injecting race into their activism or who don't feel the need to involve racial/ethnic signifiers in their veganism. In fact, we were eager to write this chapter precisely because we wanted to make clear what exactly we take black veganism to be, *which is not simply being black and being vegan* (more on this later). Among those who tell us that veganism is "all about the animals" are many people of color.

For these vegans, veganism *is* about the animals. They accept the traditional, mainstream understanding of the animal situation as having to do with speciesism, which is different from but relevantly "like" racism or sexism. They agree that the way to resist speciesism is to abstain from animal products (as much as possible) and to reject speciesist rhetoric and imagery. This resistance might be political or simply personal, or both.

However, even black vegans who agree with the mainstream vegan project many times face discriminatory behaviors and attitudes from non-black vegans. Understandably, they might feel unsafe and excluded, and seek safe spaces among those who have faced similar discrimination or with those who have allied with them, which can lead to race-specific spaces.

But this is not what we mean by "black veganism."

2. Black Veganism

In the fall of 2009, one of our friends, a self-described amateur performance artist (at the time) staged a wonderful production of Yoko Ono's
Cut Piece (1964).[1] For anyone not familiar with it, a performer is instructed
to sit on the stage with a pair of scissors placed in front of her or him. One
by one, audience members approach the performer and, using the scissors,
cut off a piece or pieces of the performer's clothing.

It was striking to see how just *changing the performer* greatly affected the
performance and what the performance meant. Each time these instruc-
tions (or "score") for *Cut Piece* are enacted, the performance is *different*
depending on the performer. The performer is *central* to the enactment
of the piece and, as such, can never be abstracted from the final product.

Our friend differed in many ways from Yoko Ono: the former is a
black American with a heavy build, living off student loans to make her
way through school; the latter is a petite Japanese woman who was an
integral member of the New York avant-garde scene. Even if both women
were intending to send the same general message with their performances,
their specific life contexts shaped not only the delivery of those messages
but affected the messages themselves.

In a sense, one could say there are merely different ways to perform
this piece, and it would be a mistake to assume that one is more legitimate than the other. Even Yoko Ono herself understood that her original
performance was not the only way to perform the piece. Her performance is her interpretation of how best to convey a particular message,
but someone with a different body size, gender, race, or lifestyle, in a
different location and time and with different capabilities and intentions,
will have his or her own interpretation of that message and their own way
of conveying it.

Our experience of *Cut Piece*, and our reflections on it over the years,
have encouraged us to see sites of activism and movements in a similar
way—as contextualized by the activists that comprise those spaces. In
other words, we want to call attention to the fact that it *matters* whether we
identify as white or black or Latina, straight or queer, atheist or Muslim,

and so on. Why does it matter? Because these things affect how we see and think about what goes on in the world. They affect how we understand, articulate, and choose to act on what is going on.

Black veganism, then, encourages activists to think about and articulate the animal situation as they see fit *through* their lived situation. Sometimes, this might even mean never addressing the exploitation and oppression of animals directly. It's a *way* of being vegan, which suggests that there are lots of equally legitimate ways to understand, articulate, and resist how it is that animals are negatively impacted by our systems of power. As the name *black veganism* suggests, we believe our identification as black affects what our veganism will look like.

3. Advantages

Many times, people assume that offering a nuanced analysis of movements, especially by highlighting our differences in our activism, fragments them. This assumption is understandable given that, in this culture, differences have always been presented to us in the context of a hierarchy. As a result, people tend to find such projects suspicious or they even demonize others when they signal some characteristic or attribute that sets them apart from others in the movement.

We take the position that nuancing our movements by explicitly pointing to the operative perspective (whether that perspective is grounded in one's racial, sexual, religious, or whatever experience) *helps* movements.

It's worth remembering that problems like the exploitation and oppression of animals have to first be put into words and then explained before we start building movements for resistance. These words—the way the problem is articulated—and the explanation for these unfortunate phenomena are not given to us by a god, "untainted" by limited, human perspectives. *People* articulate the problem, as best they can.

Just because some people decided to articulate and so understand a problem in a certain way doesn't mean they've *exhausted* ways to talk and think about or act on that problem. Maybe they didn't think to represent the problem in some way because they just don't encounter certain things in life. Or maybe it was important for them to represent the problem in some way because certain things are always present in their lives.

The more people we have thinking about a problem we really care about from many different perspectives, the more resources we have at our disposal to do something about the problem.

That's a good thing!

But when people start talking about *the* (right) way to be vegan—that it's supposed to be about animals and no one else, that race or gender or ability or whatever is a "distraction," that the inclusion of our own lived situations is "irrelevant," and so on—such people are basically privileging a *particular* viewpoint that says just that! That is, they forget that people who say those things—about what veganism is "supposed" to look like— are *people* who have their *own way* of thinking, talking, and doing something about the oppression of animals.

They forget that people, *all* people, are situated in the world in different ways and how they are situated will inform their perspective of things, whether or not they explicitly acknowledge it. Usually, the people who don't feel the need to include racial/ethnic signifiers (or other types of signifiers like their gender, orientation, or abilities) don't feel they have to since they are the norm.

Those of us who do not count as the norm, though, tend to see and think about things differently—precisely because we're marginalized, ignored, oppressed, and so on! Obviously, we inhabit very different locations in the space of power, so the world presents itself differently to us. So, for those of us adopting black veganism, we think it's crucial to mark our veganism with the marker *black*. *Black* marks the perspective we're working with when we start to think and do something about the animal situation.

This is not to say that all people—black or otherwise—who don't do this, who are happy with more mainstream and traditional articulations and activist approaches to the animal situation, are doing something wrong. We'd like to refrain from going into other spaces and telling those participants how they should see and understand things. Again, in line with lots of refreshing decolonial work being conducted all over the world today, we think activists should welcome a plurality of perspectives and approaches even if they are not quite in line with their own, or even if they do not quite understand them.

Instead of privileging only one way of talking and doing something about a problem—an inclination that erases and silences other voices in the process, by the way—why not acknowledge how our own lived situations help us reframe and re-understand the problem? Why not forge connections between the oppressions we face with the oppressions other groups face, whether human or not, in order to see the big picture? Why police each other when we could be learning from each other?

4. Conclusion

In this chapter, we've tried to clarify what we refer to as black veganism. There is a lot more to say on the matter, obviously, but for now these introductory remarks will suffice. We do not intend this clarification to be a criticism of mainstream vegan/animal advocacy movements nor do we intend to give the impression that others ought to see things as we do. We want to resist the simplistic reduction of black veganism to being black people who happen to be vegan. In doing so, we hope to have provided one reason for why race might be relevant and, in fact, integral to veganism and animal advocacy.

We wish to resist the temptation to present our perspective as universal or objective and, in order to do so, we highlight the perspective we are working with. We are not doing anything new but merely joining in a long tradition of people celebrating pluralism.

But we also hope we've shown something else as well. In the end, veganism just can't be all about the animals, no matter how much we'd like it to be. *We're* the ones who talk about and act on this problem. So, it will always have to be a little bit about us, too.

→ 10 ←

SEVEN REASONS WHY LABELS AREN'T NECESSARILY THE ROOT OF OPPRESSION

◆

Aph Ko and Syl Ko
November 16, 2015

PRINCE EA (RICHARD WILLIAMS) IS AN AMERICAN RAPPER WHO IS KNOWN for speaking out about issues centering on social justice, politics, and the environment. In 2015, he released a video titled, "I Am NOT Black, You Are NOT White,"[1] which went viral. The entire theme of the video essentially revolves around the idea that the system of racial labeling is the root cause of division in our country. In other words, racial labels like *black* or *white* are problematic because they are imposed on us and cause us to divide ourselves from one another. A mutual friend sent this video to us because he wanted to know our thoughts on it, and after watching it we felt that we needed to write an article about it, considering millions of people are unfortunately being exposed to a post-racial narrative that is seemingly progressive because it's being authored by a minoritized person. Part of the lyrics include:

> I am not Black
> I mean, that's what the world calls me, but it's not me
> I didn't come out of my mother's womb saying, "Hey everybody, I'm Black."
> No, I was taught to be black

56

And you were taught to call me that
Along with whatever you call yourself
It's just a label.

See, from birth the world force-feeds us these labels,
And eventually we all swallow them.
We digest and accept the labels, never ever doubting them.
But there's one problem:
Labels are not you and labels are not me,
Labels are just labels.
But who we truly are is not skin deep.
See, when I drive my car, no one would ever confuse the
    car for me.
Well, when I drive my body, why do you confuse me for
    my body?
It's *my* body, get it? Not me.

In our opinion, we feel this video went viral precisely because it doesn't challenge anyone to change his or her behavior. The video offers a seductive message of "sameness," where everyone is collapsed into the same category, thereby flattening out all systems of oppression and discrimination as though we should all do the same amount of work to stop hatred (despite the fact that some strategically benefit from the system, and others are crushed by it). We've broken down why we don't particularly like the message in the video, and what we think the actual problems are instead.

1. Using Labels to Define Ourselves Isn't the Problem

The majority of the world's population doesn't have access to labeling, and, thus, to choosing how they'd like to define and understand themselves. A tiny percentage has had the power to label everyone else how they see fit—making themselves superior, or the norm, and all others inferior, "the Other." That's what members of minoritized groups have been suffering from—being seen as inferior and unworthy, and being denied the dignity to define ourselves—not the act of labeling itself.

Prior to colonialism, every group of people had its own narrative system, which gave rise to unique, fundamental classifications and labels. Many times, these narratives prioritized the group that authored the system. But there was nothing problematic about this because those narratives were not globally instituted as the only legitimate way to understand or group people.

In denying legitimacy to the ways populations label themselves, the dominant group keeps hold of their power. For instance, it's no coincidence that upon arriving in the Americas, Africans were stripped of their names—our most fundamental label—and forced to assume the European names chosen by their white masters. This was a strategy to disempower Africans.

The problem isn't labeling: it's who's doing the labeling and for what purpose.

2. It's Misguided to Assume that People Wishing to Mark Their Group as Different Is Necessarily "Divisive"

Although labels, categories, and so on do have the function of distinguishing populations, as well as individuals within those populations, it's silly to assume that individuation itself creates problems. As a simple example, we divide ourselves by our first names (one of us is Syl, the other Aph), family names (the Gonzalezes, who live down the road from the Kowalskis), affiliations (we are black feminists and our good friends are indigenous feminists), or lifestyles (punks, hippies). We can establish even stronger divisions among ourselves, informed by whatever we like (yes, even physical traits) and still get along.

People assume differences must be bad or divisive because we've always served up differences within hierarchical logic. But we tend to overlook the possibility that wanting to homogenize people—despite our different histories, rituals, lifestyles, locations, and ways of thinking—might itself be an oppressive project.

3. We're So Tired of People Saying Race Isn't Real Just Because It Isn't Biologically or Materially "Real"

You know what else isn't biologically real? Principles of justice. Moral systems. Romantic love. These are just things we humans made up. But that doesn't mean the only criterion for reality is biology or the material world. Things can be *socially* real and those things usually matter *the most* to us—precisely because *we* made them up.

4. Emphasizing Similarities Won't Help the Oppressed

As we said in chapter 7: "Racism, however, draws on the *created*, raced body. So, although it might help the racist cause to stress differences between groups, emphasizing similarities won't do much to alleviate racism."

Showing how everyone is the "same" bypasses the whole problematic system of white supremacy, patriarchy, and so on, which tells us that certain people have more value than others. To ignore those systems (which caused these problems) and chalk it up to mere labels absolutely misses the mark when it comes to understanding how oppression operates and is sustained.

5. To Tackle Systems of Oppression, Your Activism Must Be Guided by Your Social Location in the System

Oppressed people and privileged people shouldn't be engaging in the same *exact* efforts to end the system. It makes absolutely no sense for everyone to do identical things to end systems that disproportionately impact everyone. Also, Prince Ea fails to realize that privileged folks don't necessarily want the system to end because they benefit from it.

In his song, Prince Ea states:

> Let me break it down
> See, our bodies are just cars that we operate and drive
>   around,
> The dealership will call society decided to label mine the
>   "black edition,"

Yours the "Irish" or "White edition,"
And with no money down, 0% APR, and no test drive,
We were forced to own these cars for the rest of our lives.
Forgive me, but I fail to see the logic or pride
In defining myself or judging another by the cars we drive.
Because who we truly are, is found inside.

Society didn't *arbitrarily* decide to mark Prince Ea's blackness as inferior; systems of oppression like white supremacy *purposefully* did that. That's why the *black* label is viewed as "less than" and *white* isn't, so it makes no sense to act as though the *black* and *white* labels are both equally destructive simply because they're labels. If we're going to use the car analogy to describe how the system operates, the reality is some cars are *purposefully given* higher value by the car dealership based upon their color.

Additionally, assuming racial groups need to work "equally" hard to end hatred is misguided and inevitably ends up making people of color labor even harder when we're already trying to survive under these unjust systems. We do not have an equal start on the racetrack of life, meaning that we can't act as though all of our bodies are magically equal when systems of domination exist.

We would urge everyone to check out the video created by Kimberlé Crenshaw called "The Unequal Opportunity Race" for further analysis on this topic.[2]

6. Pretending Racial Terms Don't Exist
Causes More Harm than Good

We can't pretend racial notions do not exist. This could be a disastrous, even dangerous, method to employ. It does nothing to address the fact of racism and, in fact, can help maintain it.

For instance, although US laws do not make any explicit reference to races anymore, they are just as effective in maintaining racism. Racism transcends not just skin color but even racial terms themselves. Avoiding these key terms as an uprooting strategy is to misunderstand the nature of words and notions and how deeply entrenched they are in our attitudes, practices, and institutions, whether or not we explicitly refer to them.

In addition, some references to racial identification have been crucial to dismantling racism. For instance, movements in which the word *black* has been *redefined* or *reclaimed* by populations negatively impacted by racism serve to powerfully confront the messages spread by racial thinking.

7. Being "Positive" Won't Change Systems of Oppression

Remember that Pharrell Williams' song "Happy," which played on repeat on the radio for months? There's this forced narrative of happiness in our society that tells people (especially people of color) that we should be happy and laugh everything off. If you keep a positive attitude, you will be fine. If you're in a bad mood, or angry, it's because you *individually* chose to be in a bad mood! *Stop letting the world get to you!!*

Black folks like Pharrell Williams and Prince Ea are basically creating white-centric artistic messages that are designed to function as sedatives for black rage.[3] Minorities are the ones that are tasked with singing *kumbaya* with white folks, or else we're being "angry." If we decide to call ourselves "black," we're dividing ourselves from others. Right. . . .

Prince Ea is basically saying: *If you experience racism, it's because you're allowing yourself to be upset about a label that isn't even real, bruh!*

He ends his video with a group of diverse folks standing around with the word LOVE in front of them. Sure, we should all have love for one another, but part of the reason why we don't isn't because individual people are just mean and hateful. It's because we have violent systems of oppression that folks of color don't control and that Prince Ea doesn't mention once. (He'd probably say that white supremacy is just a label.)

It's violent to stop folks of color from expressing their justified rage. Compassion shouldn't be a one-way street where black folks are "kind" to white folks and work alongside them to end systems that are killing them, as though we are all *equally* being crushed under this system. Compassion is allowing black folks to be angry. Real love is when privileged folks stop assuming world peace will happen in a white supremacist, patriarchal society that strategically disenfranchises certain bodies.

11

WE'VE RECLAIMED BLACKNESS NOW IT'S TIME TO RECLAIM "THE ANIMAL"

(Part II of "Addressing Racism Requires Addressing the Situation of Animals")

◆

Syl Ko
December 15, 2015

[K]nowledge of the human is . . . obtained not through projected images of the self, but through attention to the deracializing and decolonizing actions of entrapped modern selves.—**Nelson Maldonado-Torres**[1]

UNTIL I WAS TWENTY-ONE YEARS OLD, I WAS EMBARRASSED TO BE BLACK. I remember someone telling me that I resembled a (beautiful!) black athlete, after which I ran to my room and cried the whole night. From the first grade to my final semester in college, I would stop participating in class when we got to the transatlantic slave trade or when it was Black History Month. I religiously straightened my curly, kinky hair and would say that was the way it grew out of my head. I was known for my vehement hostility to dating and marriage, but really it was a disguise for my conviction that no one would ever find me lovable because, according to every film and TV show I had ever seen, men, even non-white men, preferred white-looking women. If you asked me the dreaded "What *are* you?" question, I'd reply with the equally dreaded, "I'm half-white and half-black but *really* I'm just [my white father's ethnicity]." I was even a hardcore Republican. (Sorry, world!)

Of course, my story is not every black or brown person's story. But the truth is that, for a very long time, I hated myself because of my race.

Lots of times, when racism is discussed in the media, or in activism, or even in spaces dedicated to promoting "diversity," the bulk of the attention is on how white individuals/populations treat racialized individuals or populations. Interestingly, in presenting the issue in this manner, we tend to neglect what makes racism so pernicious for those of us negatively affected by it.

For many, if not most, black folks (not to mention other non-white people), racism is especially detrimental because we experience ourselves as *fundamentally* "less than," as an ontological defect. The feeling of this *lack* manifests itself in a variety of ways: hatred of the features that make us recognizably "black," wanting to distance ourselves from our history as slaves or colonized peoples out of shame, a general mode of disengagement from our peers and surroundings when having to exist in white spaces or among predominantly white people, and so on.[2]

This lack is almost never mentioned in mainstream discourses on the problem of racism. Ironically, in our well-intentioned discussions about racism and "diversity," we continue the racist tradition of *overlooking* the perspectives of people who suffer from it. As a result, the focus is almost exclusively on bringing non-white, but especially black, populations into white spaces and on "growing" their rights and equal status.[3]

However, as psychiatrist Alvin Poussaint points out, "[Black people] are not just seeking equality, full rights and freedom. What's going on now is also a search and fight for an *inner* emancipation from the effects of white racism—to become somehow internally *purged*. So, it's not just a question of moving freely in white society."[4]

Sometimes people (again, with good intentions) suggest we ought to refrain from referring to ourselves as "black" or from assuming racial labels altogether as a way to dislodge racism. For instance, the video "I Am

NOT Black, You Are NOT White" created by rapper Prince Ea (discussed in chapter 10), supports this type of strategy. But, again, this approach reproduces a narrative about racism that completely dismisses the *inner* struggle that black people face, a struggle that cannot be eliminated by merely avoiding racial terms. Racism is not merely discursive—it is *embodied* and *felt* in those it marks as inferior.[5]

W. E. B. Du Bois stated, in response to a student who protested the use of the word *Negro* by black people:

> Would the Negro problem be suddenly and eternally settled [if the name *Negro* could be changed to something else]? Would you be any less ashamed of being descended from a black man, or would your schoolmates feel any less superior to you? . . . Your real work, my dear young man, does not lie with names. It is not a matter of changing them, losing them, or forgetting them. . . . The feeling of inferiority is in you, not in any name. The name merely evokes what is already there. Exorcise the hateful complex and no name can ever make you hang your head."[6]

As we all know given our rich history of what I'll broadly refer to as "black pride" movements, Du Bois was not the only person to have this insight.[7] Many black activists put into action what seemed to many to be a counterintuitive plan: to resist and fight racism and racialization in general, we need to reappropriate "blackness" or what it means to be "black."

Many of us have been calling for a return to this approach. I think these kinds of movements, which sought to reclaim blackness, are tremendously powerful. It is one of the few strategies that addresses the more routine aspects of the anti-racist struggle (rights, equality, and so on), while also successfully doing something about the primary aspect of this struggle: healing the bruised and wounded psyches of black populations.

Although I am in favor of this strategy, however, I'd like to speak to one major revision that must be made if it is to be successful in actually dismantling racism: to complete the project, we must go one step further and reclaim the notion of "the animal." If we do not take this final step, we will make the common mistake of confusing the map for the territory.[8]

To make sense of my proposed revision, let's think about what it would mean to reclaim "the animal" from the more routine perspective of racism (as a matter of growing rights and achieving equality) and then from the primary, lived perspective of racism (as a matter of the internal struggle).

From the Routine Perspective of Racism

Caribbean scholar and cultural theorist Sylvia Wynter notes that our current conception of the human/humanity is a Eurocentric invention. Although there have been countless ways of expressing human activity throughout history, the *model* we take for humankind is the one devised by colonial Western Europe. On this model, there is *the* human (white, Western male with the ideal human counterpart: the white, Western female) and "its human Others—that is, Indians, Negroes, Natives[9] [and, I would add, Jews and Muslims]."

What separates the "human Others" from the Ideal Human and what distinguishes the human Others from each other is their ranking on the human–animal scale. In chapter 4, I pointed out that I don't think it's apparent to most of us that the notions of "human" and "animal" are racially constituted. The racial hierarchy tracks not just a color descent but also a species descent. At the top of the hierarchy sits the white male human and at the bottom sits the shady and *necessarily opposite* figure of "the animal." These two poles signify two contrary moral statuses—the closer your category is to the white male human, the more you "matter." The closer your category is to the shady, vague "animal," the less you "matter."

Whether or not we explicitly use this language or instead use code words that coincide with it, such as "subpersons," "nonhumans," "inhuman," and so on, doesn't matter. What is relevant here is that the organizing principle for racial logic lies in the human–animal divide, wherein the human and the animal are understood to be *moral opposites*.

That means that what gives rise to these racial categories and racial thinking is a particular understanding of what a human being *is*. A human being is *fundamentally* opposite to animals (with "animals" here being a gross reduction of a vast plurality of species, of course). With these poles set in place—the former as extreme superiority and the latter as extreme inferiority—those who authored this system placed *themselves* in the former position and from there divided humanity along a spectrum that went all the way "down" to "the animal."

This model of the human is still in use today.

So, in black reappropriation movements, activists effectively begin to disrupt the modern, imperialistic understanding of humanity. But because they leave the *foundation* untouched, the dismantling can never be complete. We need to go beyond the racial categories and subvert their anchor: the human–animal divide.

In short, then, what condemns us to our inferior status, even before we can speak or act is not merely our racial category but *that* our racial category is marked *the most* by animality. Its proximity to animality signals inferiority. We certainly don't want to affirm the current conception of humanity by trying to distance ourselves from animality. And we certainly don't want to pretend these terms don't exist. The best strategy is to reclaim in order to disrupt, and then to de-link from the narrative altogether.

From the Primary, Lived Perspective of Racism

Reappropriation of "the animal" from this perspective is about reclaiming the animal within us.

Now, I don't mean to imply what some other philosophers are keen on suggesting, which is that beneath our linguistic, rational selves lie primitive animalistic attributes and tendencies, which we share with most nonhuman animals.[10] These philosophers believe that such an argument is one way to get us thinking about our obligations to animals. Namely, they believe that it is due to the false representation of our species as purely rational, moral, language-based, and so on—and the repression of our "animal side"—that we tend to ignore the plight of nonhuman animals.

67

Although views like these are interesting, they *accept* the notion of animality as offered by mainstream, Eurocentric thinking as exclusively pertaining to nonhuman animals. In this view, animals are impulsive, irrational, "primitive," _____ (fill in the blank with basic generalizations of animals).

Instead, I hold that racialized populations, particularly black people, view themselves from the borders of the human–animal divide. It is clear to most of us that "animality" is not exhausted by reference to nonhuman animals but that *we* share in it as well, by virtue of our perceived and felt "less than" status. The feeling of the *lack* comes from the animal within. The animal is smuggled in with the black. Or, put more accurately, the animal within makes *possible* the black within.

The animal is not *separate* from our "blackness." It is a part of it.

That said, we generally refer to this phenomenon in reference to race alone. This makes sense given the mainstream, Eurocentric construals of animality and race as independent of one another. But by talking about our feeling of ontological *lack* from the perspective of "the animal within," we can connect race to animality to reflect the true nature of anti-black racism/oppression.

Reclaiming blackness, then, will require going a little deeper and reclaiming animality as well. If we are going to reconfigure and understand blackness on our own terms, we must also do this with the notion of "the animal."

OK, but What Does All of this Mean, Really?

First, I am endorsing the approach of reappropriation to resisting and fighting racism. This means we ought to assume our stance not by fighting or distancing ourselves from our racial label, but by refusing to adhere to the white-is-superior/black-is-inferior logic simply by *living in a way to affirm its opposite*. Reappropriation projects, then, are not just about talking or theorizing differently. It is a real, lived praxis.

Secondly, I suggest that *from within this mindset* we also need to reclaim the notion of "the animal." The current conception of "the animal" belongs to the narrative that supplied us with the current, racist, sexist, everything-ist conception of "the human." In this problematic narrative, the human and the animal are *necessary opposites*. The whole reason we have all of these horrible racial categories is because of *this* underlying logic surrounding the oppositional moral relationship between the human and the animal. In reclaiming "the animal," we thereby refuse to accept that there is a morally relevant conceptual difference between the category "human" and the vague category of "animal."

Thirdly, this process has real implications for those who suffer the most from the category of "the animal"—nonhuman animals. If we reclaim "the animal" in the same way that we've reclaimed blackness, we acknowledge that nonhuman animals, too, are among the many beings who are condemned by the current system. Their inferiority is also materially located, in their bodies, which are generally marked as consumption items, objects to be used as we see fit, and so forth.

With my proposed revision, we generate a certain commitment to animals *from within* an anti-racist commitment. We ought to refuse to treat animals as objects to which we owe no obligations. "It's just an animal" can no longer be an excuse for treating a being as if s(he) merely existed for us. To think in that way is to participate in racial thinking—the very kind of thinking this project intends to dissolve.[11]

12

NOTES FROM THE BORDER
OF THE HUMAN–ANIMAL DIVIDE

Thinking and Talking about Animal Oppression
When You're Not Quite Human Yourself

◆

Syl Ko
January 13, 2016

> The struggle is inner: Chicano, indio, American Indian, mojado, mexicano, immigrant Latino, Anglo in power, working class Anglo, Black, Asian—our psyches resemble the bordertowns and are populated by the same people. The struggle has always been inner, and is played out in the outer terrains. Awareness of our situation must come before inner changes, which in turn come before changes in society. Nothing happens in the "real" world unless it first happens in the images in our heads.
> —Gloria Anzaldúa[1]

> [T]here is no essence; there is only history—living history.
> —Aimé Césaire[2]

IT'S FUNNY THE WAY WE'RE ENCOURAGED TO THINK ABOUT THE DEPLORABLE situation of animals. We are supposed to think of animals as their own, discrete class, which faces a unique sort of oppression. Like all other movements, we animal advocates are supposed to make a space devoted specifically to this class of beings and their struggle. What the animals face is relevantly *like* other "isms," and many of us are hard at work revealing these "connections." But the likeness ends there: oppressions are "connected" but, at the end of the day, this is speciesism we're talking about: something that is peculiar to animals. And that's that.

There is something bizarre to me about racialized people and other marginalized folks who are advocates for animals going along with this line of thinking. I'm not saying that all of us who are marginalized ought to have exactly the same ideas about how to carry out our animal advocacy. But it's interesting that we are supposed to follow some sort of "model" for how we ought to think about animal oppression that, coincidentally (or maybe, conveniently), rules out our own experiences of being oppressed *ourselves*.[3]

The idea that there must be a movement that specifically devotes itself to animals alone and that there is something "progressive" about showing how this space "links" or "connects" with other types of oppression completely ignores the very problems oppressed humans have been facing when it comes to talking about all of the other "isms." If anti-racism is devoted to dismantling racism, and feminism is devoted to dismantling sexism, and the LGBTQ+ movements are devoted to dismantling heteronormativity (among other things!), and environmentalism is meant to dismantle and so on . . . , then you can see why many of us are torn as to where we fit in our own liberation struggles. This problem intensifies when we notice that each space is governed by its own logic, which many times perpetuate other "isms."

That's not to say that finding one's place can't be done; I know many people who do it. But it comes at a significant cost to our well-being and it's draining: we have to navigate racism in one space, sexism in another, face ridicule in environmentalist spaces, and so on and so on.[4] Sometimes, putting up with this state of affairs can even make us give up and accept the status quo.

What hasn't occurred to many of us is that this model of compartmentalizing oppressions tracks the problematic Eurocentric compartmentalization of the world and its members in general. For many of us, this compartmentalized way of thinking and talking is crucial to erasing us altogether. For instance, in her outstanding article "Toward a Decolonial Feminism," philosopher María Lugones notes: "If woman and black are terms for homogenous, atomic, separable categories, then their intersection shows us the absence of black women rather than their presence. So, to see non-white women is to exceed 'categorical' logic. . . . I want to emphasize categorical, dichotomous, hierarchical logic as central to modern, colonial, capitalist thinking about race, gender and sexuality."[5] In addition, this compartmentalized way of thinking and talking downplays the intimate relations between seemingly different oppressions we all face. "Links" and "intersections" and "connections" are clumsy tools when dealing with inextricably entangled phenomena that are not merely "connected" but all make up the same territory.

That's why I think those of us who reside in, think, speak, theorize about, and exist on what I call the border of "the human" and "the animal" play a special role when it comes to the situation of animals.

Part of that role includes a more responsible way of representing the interests of animals. There is a large literature on the issue of speaking on behalf of or "speaking for" oppressed individuals that belong to a group that is not "your own"—a subject that is often raised when it comes to animal advocacy.[6]

It's not that we're trying to make ourselves primary in a movement that's not "supposed" to be about us. (Who decided what the movement is "supposed" to be about, anyway?! Isn't the nature of the movement precisely what's under debate?) Rather, animals' fates and their situation are very much entangled in our own. I don't mean this in the broad sense in which we are *all* animals biologically. Thinking of ourselves as biologically related might make us feel connected to animals in special ways, but not in the sense that we need to fight on their behalf. You can feel connected to animals, but that doesn't necessarily mean anything follows from that feeling. Slave masters might feel genuinely connected to their slaves or abusers might feel connected to their battered partners and children; as we all know, the mere feeling of a connection doesn't guarantee the right kind of action. You can see yourself as biologically related to beings without this bringing any further feelings of unity or obligation toward them. For instance, colonizers knew they were biologically related to the colonized people but, if anything, this only increased the number of ways the former exploited the latter.

When I say our situation—the situation of not-quite-humans—and animal oppression are entangled, I mean something deeper. Our position in society—our social, political, and moral status—is rooted in the domain of the Other.

This is a much stronger bond to which we can appeal. It's not grounded in biology (biology never gave us any moral directions) but relies on the very matter we are bringing to light: our "less than" status in society and how it is the result of a long project of domination.

Nonhumans, subhumans, not-quite-humans (fill in your favorite inferior label)—however you refer to us: we are all props for a narrative about "the human," a small group of people that are not just homo sapiens but an ideal *type* of homo sapiens.

When we think about our oppressions with respect to their cause—the propping up of "the human" (the long project of Western colonialism and domination)—then the fine-grained differences between them start to matter less. Racism, sexism, ableism, speciesism, classism, and so on: these are real phenomena, of course. But as Sylvia Wynter warns, we should avoid mistaking the "maps" for the "territory." The territory is this massive domain of Others, whose scope can only be grasped when we dig deeper beyond the constraints of the specific "isms" and see ourselves—following Frantz Fanon's words—as *damned* beings by virtue of our lacking a full "human" status.

The extent of this territory is at once scary but also encouraging. We are a universe of our own—this domain of Others.

That means, in spite of our cosmetic differences and situations—our many species, races, genders, belief systems, ways of being, geographic regions of origin—we are kindred spirits in a fight to depose "the human."

I am saying all of this to show you the power and strength we can find in being aware of our not-quite-human status (in those terms) and that, in embracing it, we find we must break away from the standard ways of talking about the situation of animals. Where we are positioned along the human–animal divide ought to matter when it comes to thinking about animal oppression because, for those of us along the border, this is part and parcel of *our* oppression.

Our specific locations on this border might differ, depending on whether we are there because we are racialized especially as black or brown; or because we practice the "wrong" kind of faith and possess "inferior" spiritual beliefs; or because we are indigenous; or because we lack certain abilities or a certain kind of body; or because we don't quite meet gender expectations; or because of our region of origin or class. As most of us know, this list can go on and on.

But these differences are negligible in the grand scheme of things because all that matters is that there are "humans" and then all of "human's" Others. And when we Others act as carriers for "human" values, and in doing so reproduce their injustices among ourselves, we lose sight of the real issue and how we got here in the first place. We have to keep our eye on the prize: a "[break] with the imperialist ontology and meta-physical essentialism of Enlightenment man."[7]

Of course, we face an uphill battle. I don't mean this solely in the sense of navigating the world as beings who are racialized, gendered, queer, and so forth. I also mean it in the sense that we will be laughed at, ignored, accused of being irrational, made to be irrelevant, and so on by taking on this very different way of being advocates for animals. After all, only humans are taken seriously. Only humans get to be heard. Only humans are contributors and . . . well, we're not quite human. Our perspectives, theories, positions, and assumptions will be cast as jokes. Our views will always be "less than," non-standard, mere alternatives to "the canon."[8]

Again, we should see this situation as working to our advantage. Let's use our exclusion and invisibility as a power to create impermeable spaces for ourselves, unburdened by the ridiculous and biased premises of the dominant class. Let's use our erasure from this rotten-to-the-core

Western notion of humanity to build up a different "new world," one that is not defined in terms of dichotomies or hierarchies or emotional death—but centered on love: one in which we accept ambiguity and difference, grounded in an expansive, limitless "we."

We are at the center of a radical shift taking place in pro-animal discourse precisely because, upon self-reflection, we can see that our struggle is their struggle. I don't mean this symbolically. I mean this literally.

We are realizing that by existing in this strange, liminal space, the space of being not-quite-human, we are forced to reconceive and reject the standard articulation of what speciesism *is* and how to fight it. In recognizing our strange status explicitly in terms of the grand division that makes all "isms" possible, the human–animal dichotomy, we voluntarily align ourselves with our fellow beings, those who do not belong to homo sapiens, in solidarity as we all somehow continue to thrive despite the crushing weight of the figure "the human."

13

VEGANS OF COLOR AND RESPECTABILITY POLITICS

*When Eurocentric Veganism Is Used
to Rehabilitate Minorities*

◆

*Aph Ko
January 29, 2016*

NOW THAT THE MAINSTREAM IS SLOWLY TAKING NOTICE OF BLACK AND brown vegans (because some folks are legitimately excited about this and others are realizing that it's marketable), a new, albeit predictable, trend is popping up. Because of the mainstream reductive framing of black veganism as merely black people planting gardens and advocating for animal rights in a white-centric way (rather than a sociopolitical movement that rearticulates black oppression through the lens of animality and race), an unfortunate air of respectability politics is emerging from mainstream stories about black vegans and other vegans of color.

Because mainstream veganism is saturated with Eurocentric logic, the assumption is that black folks who go vegan are "transcending" their negative situations, not only in terms of their health, but also in terms of their racial location.

In particular, the mainstream seems to be *obsessing* over former black "gang members" going vegan or "gangsters" who are now vegan. Guerrilla gardeners like Ron Finley (known as the Gangsta Gardener) are fighting white supremacy in creative ways, despite the fact that they don't explicitly say this. However, Finley's story is being decontextualized and reframed through a narrative that makes the dominant class comfortable. *See—these black folks aren't lazy! If more black folks were like this, their communities would be cleaner and they wouldn't be living in poverty!*

However, Ron didn't create his guerrilla gardening projects for fun. He's fighting a white-supremacist capitalist system that has shoved certain bodies into communities where access to fresh foods and affordable healthcare is scarce. Actually, it's sad that black people need to plant gardens on curbs because our government is nutritionally starving them. This is an epidemic that goes hand in hand with communities in Flint, Michigan, having to drink poisoned water. This isn't a romantic, "feel good" story. This is fucked up—plain and simple.

There's something ironic about a man like Ron Finley—who plants gardens in spaces white supremacy created to nutritionally and intellectually starve minorities—being celebrated by the mainstream white news media. The goal of guerrilla gardening isn't to make black folks look more peaceful and benevolent; it's to engage in a new type of fight in which we are taking care of ourselves in an era that's actively trying to poison and kill us. It's an act of survival.

It's great that people like Ron and other urban farmers are engaging with DIY, grassroots activism to fight back. However, we need to watch *how* we frame their stories and most importantly, we need to watch out for *who* is framing these stories.

Some white vegan media spaces like to circulate stories centering on black gang members who are now vegan and peaceful, which are currently being used to show the "mainstream" how black people *can* be civilized, nurturing, productive, and peaceful, especially at a time when the dominant class is panicking because of Black Lives Matter protests and riots. Nonetheless, the framing of these stories coincidentally leaves out any mention of white supremacy, capitalism, and systemic racism, which is why these folks are in gangs in the first place and why they are forced to garden on curbs and in other nontraditional spaces.

This rhetoric reeks of black-on-black crime nostalgia as though black folks are individually responsible for "cleaning up" crime-filled communities that they seemingly created, even though these spaces are products of systemic racism and classism. The responsibility is still on the minorities. In other words, the framing of these stories casts black people as both the problem and the solution, which is problematic considering there are systems that strategically disenfranchise certain populations.

There's something infantilizing about the framing of these black-vegan stories and spotlights. It reminds me of people who chalk up black-on-black crime to "fatherless" men[1] rather than systemic racism and generations' worth of racial terrorism. Black men are seemingly "acting out" because "their fathers are absent." Similarly, black vegans who were former gang members are framed through a narrative of transformation and maturation as though they were merely dangerous, irresponsible black children before, and now they're respectable, civilized, grown adults who are individually "transcending" racial stereotypes because they made the individual choice to go vegan and plant gardens. In fact, a lot of black vegans speak of using veganism to become the best "versions of themselves," conjuring up a notion of individual transcendence through neoliberal politics.

Eurocentric Veganism Is Framed as a Therapeutic Corrective to Racism

Because veganism is still associated with whiteness, there's a myth that says vegans are (conveniently) peaceful, nonviolent, intelligent, and evolved, which is why minorities who go vegan are treated as if they've transcended their race. The reframing of "gang member" to "gardener" is saturated with a racialized narrative.

This reality is generally why I dislike comedy videos that display nonvegan minorities trying vegan foods for the first time, because they are always wrapped up in racialized stereotypes. You can find an example of this on YouTube. *We are mitú* has a video titled, "Cholos Try Vegan Food: Kale Chips and Kombucha." The whole storyline relies on tropes of violence and drug use to show just how backward these particular folks are since they can't identify the healthy foods. In fact, all of these Latino "gangsters" assume that the kale is marijuana. Despite the fact that the video is outlined through an overt comedic lens, and even appears to be catering to a specific audience who might know that the humor is satirical, the video still naturalizes a troublesome point: that lacking familiarity with healthful foods is supposed to be funny. Veganism is far removed from these individuals' everyday discourse and they are framed as unintelligent, infantile, and criminal.

Because minorities are viewed as subhuman, watching these folks try healthy vegan foods (read: white-people foods) is depicted comically in a manner reminiscent of a chimpanzee wearing a tuxedo. Both scenarios are framed as emulating "ideal homo sapiens" (read: white humans) and miserably failing, naturalizing their supposed inferiority and the superiority of those in power.

The vegans of color who *are* celebrated are the ones who don't racially rock the boat. So long as we plant gardens and advocate for animals outside of an *explicit* politicization of white supremacy, we are fine; when we start to create our own movements and theories that take into account our racial experiences within white supremacist capitalism, then we are attacked.

Unsurprisingly, veganism and animal rights are domains that white elites consider their own, which is why they incessantly feel the need to insert their comments into our spaces when our projects have absolutely nothing to do with them. They approve of the Ron Finleys of the world and, in the next breath, chastise the Syl Kos and Breeze Harpers of the world, who are actively trying to articulate a vegan politics that doesn't conflict with their experiences of racialized oppression.

Since veganism is culturally associated with whiteness, there's an unfortunate narrative of racial transcendence for minority folks who embrace the vegan lifestyle. So, when we *still* insert our racial experiences even *after* we embrace veganism, the self-proclaimed leaders are confused: *What does race have to do with veganism? We let you into this space where you won't have the baggage of racial stereotypes!*

In fact, many from the dominant class get offended when we speak of our racial oppression as a phenomenon that's entangled with animal oppression, because through veganism the white elites seemingly gave us a new black citizenship, a refuge from racial prejudice, a passport of sorts to a new "post-racial" landscape. By conjuring up "race" again in this new territory, we are displaying signs that we're not "fully" rehabilitated.

Veganism shouldn't be a tool the dominant class uses to rehabilitate blackness, as though blackness is inherently criminal, deviant, and barbaric.

The consistent focus on former gang members turned vegan perpetuates this narrative that veganism is peaceful and automatically leads to social justice. Veganism is sold as the perfect antidote to years of systemic racism.

* * *

I'm writing this piece as conversations about the overwhelming whiteness of the American Academy of Motion Picture Arts and Sciences awards (the Oscars) is taking place and I would like to connect the two issues.

Black people who are interested in authoring their own, unique stories and who want to produce new narratives about black life aren't honored. The black filmmakers who *are* celebrated are the ones who share stories about slavery, black death, or overtly racial themes that make white elites feel comfortable. White folks don't mind black people talking about "race" so long as (a) white people still get to control the overall narrative and (b) white people aren't explicitly held responsible.

Similarly, vegan stories that continue this narrative of poor-black-person-struggling-to-survive-and-be-better (with no explicit mention of white supremacy) are shared and celebrated because those in power are erased from the story line. This is in part why I've observed that white elites celebrate black *food-justice* activists who point to *food access* as the main issue facing minorities within the vegan landscape; black vegan theorists and anti-racists who point to white supremacy as the problem aren't celebrated as widely. Projects that center on food access and food justice don't rhetorically rock the racial boat; those who seek to display the supremacy of the white human as the crux of the problem are ostracized and humiliated.

As soon as black folks want to create new vegan theories or models with which to articulate animal oppression or new intellectual projects to cater to underserved audiences, we're chastised by white elites and ridiculed because they aren't the main authors of the project. Of course, within both Hollywood slave films as well as vegan stories about guerrilla gardeners or rehabilitated gang members, white supremacy is conveniently pushed to the back. We can easily talk about Ron Finley and guerrilla gardeners without mentioning white supremacy. We can easily talk about food deserts without mentioning capitalism or whiteness—and that makes everyone comfortable.

Ron and other black folks who are framed as being "rehabilitated" through veganism are held up as examples for all other black folks to follow. This is cosmetic diversity at its most exemplary: black faces are advertised and white authors are writing the story. Eurocentric logic attempts to frame Ron as a modern-day Martin Luther King Jr. figure, who is seemingly peaceful and calm, without the audience realizing that his shovel is his weapon, not a marker of his subservience.

We need to stop expecting Eurocentric veganism to correct systemic racism. We need to let the oppressed folks articulate their own movements using their own voices. The self-proclaimed leaders need to stop trying to find their next Martin Luther King Jr. to manipulate black folks into being calm and "civilized" since what Ron and other guerrilla gardeners are doing has nothing to do with being peaceful and everything to do with survival and protest. Black folks who are vegan are a threat to white supremacy, not a subset of the depoliticized white-vegan movement.

→ 14 ←

WE CAN AVOID THE DEBATE ABOUT COMPARING HUMAN AND ANIMAL OPPRESSIONS, IF WE SIMPLY MAKE THE RIGHT CONNECTIONS

◆

Syl Ko
February 4, 2016

[Mestizaje] and hybridity are celebrated, "out there", but neither [researcher] let[s] their epistemic frame get infected and mixed, like the blood and the mind of the bodies they are analyzing.—**Gloria Anzaldúa**[1]

LAST WEEK, MY SISTER AND I WERE DISCUSSING SOME OF THE VARIOUS DRAMAS unfolding in animal advocacy circles and the animal rights movement as a whole. I diagnosed these events as having very little to do with animal oppression and everything to do with who gets to produce knowledge. For instance, I've noticed many wonderful and well-intentioned activists are weighing in on the raging "debate" about whether or not it is ever OK to compare the oppression of animals to the oppression of humans (where, for once, "humans" here usually refers to black populations).

Since a slew of clueless, though well-intentioned activists repeatedly share graphic images and frighteningly empty slogans about the connections between animal slavery and human slavery (usually they mean the transatlantic slave trade from the ol' days), any and all discussions that incorporate animals and oppressed humans, especially black people, in the same space are now forbidden at the risk of a collective meltdown.[2]

If this kind of debate is any indication of the depth of the contemporary animal rights movement, if these are the kinds of connections we're fighting one another (and the public) to make, then our movement is doomed. And if these are the terms by which we have to discuss whether or not the strategy of "comparing" is worthwhile, then I can see why people on the outside refuse to take us seriously.

Generally, the debate turns on the "sensitivity" of oppressed populations about this issue and this is usually the central talking point. I'd like to move the focus (and blame) away from the "sensitivities" of certain populations and point to what I take the real problem to be.

Now, let me point out the standard way of thinking that might underpin such a debate. It's easily demonstrated by the two following observations I've made:

(1) Activists are very resistant to talking about the phenomenon of racial oppression, for instance, alongside talking about the phenomenon of speciesism. They may acknowledge that racial oppression exists and may even think it's "bad"; in fact, some might even *experience* racial oppression firsthand. But in vegan/animal rights spaces and in vegan/animal rights organizing they believe it should be "all about the animals." After all, anti-racism has many of its own spaces; vegan spaces are not the ones designed to address the problem of racism. Animals are not victims of racism. So, talk about racial oppression in these spaces is irrelevant.

(2) According to the volume of critical messages I receive by email about the view I'm developing, most activists are very resistant to and even disturbed by *theorizing* racial oppression alongside animal oppression. Interestingly, these messages are never written by people *offended* by this sort of theorizing *on behalf of racialized populations*. Rather, they are offended that animals

"can't even get their own space" in theories devoted to examining speciesism.[3]

What this tells me is that in mainstream or standard articulations of animal oppression/speciesism, we actually theoretically and discursively *encourage* a gap between human and animal oppressions, which then creates a need to try to superficially *close* this gap, and misguided people think this can be done by presenting crudely drawn and elementary images or analogies of oppression.[4] Not only are these types of comparisons or connections absurd—even worse, these simplistic characterizations miss the ways in which these struggles and these wounded subjectivities relate to one another.

In other words, those who are most eager to juxtapose these kinds of images or discuss how animal slavery is relevantly "like" human (black) slavery many times are the same people who tend to be dismissive of or resistant to views in which animal oppression and human oppression are *thought about together* and *in the same spaces* with the aim of taking to task racism, sexism, speciesism, ableism, and so on—or coloniality in general—*in tandem*.

It's no surprise that the general public isn't buying it (and are offended by it for various good reasons). Most *animal rights activists don't really believe it*, regardless of how many times they reproduce superficial slogans of alleged comparisons and connections.

So, although this debate continues to play out in terms of whether or not making these comparisons or connections is offensive, I think it obscures a far more interesting point we should be discussing: this debate only makes sense on the assumption that we continue to understand speciesism as independent and animal-specific and, as such, a phenomenon that *requires* connection to other struggles.

What I mean is this: the connecting work is happening too late in the game and for disingenuous reasons. We actually need to *believe* these things are related and convey this at the theoretical level several steps before we organize and take to the streets. The drawing together of these struggles needs to happen at those meetings and organizing lunches when people are saying "It's only about the animals!"—when we are deciding ways to *think* about and *understand* animal oppression. We need to shift how we think before we decide what kind of imagery and which words to add to our signs.

Now, what could theorizing these struggles together look like? And wouldn't this encounter the "debate" again but merely at an earlier stage?

I think one easy (although not the only) way to do this is to follow the lead of many activists, thinkers, scholars, artists, teachers, and others who draw attention to the racialized and geo-specific notion of "humanity" or "the human." This means taking seriously the feelings many of us have that we are basically nonhuman humans or, as I like to call us, not-quite-humans, and letting this be the entry point to how we think about oppression in general, as well as other things. Let me reiterate Walter Mignolo's point, which I quoted in chapter 4: "During the European renaissance, man [*sic*] was conceived at the intersection of his body and his mind, his body proportion and his intellect. Leonardo da Vinci's Vitruvian Man translated into visual language what humanists were portraying in words." As a result, "when the idea and the category of man came into the picture, it came already with a privilege."[5]

I've noticed that many of the committed and thoughtful activists who interpret humanity/the human as a *status* or *symbol* that codes particular races, subjectivities, and particular geographical locations as superior tend to include *animals* and even other members of our environment among nonhuman humans as *subjugated* by this narrative. This connection is extremely encouraging given these activists usually don't even have animals or other beings in our environment *specifically* in mind. Nonetheless, they recognize that this general phenomenon of humanity/the human hurts these beings as well.

On the flip side, mainstream animal studies, critical animal studies, animal ethics, and ordinary activists tend to talk about humanity/the human exhaustively in *biological terms*. There is no mention of humanity's other victims. Entire theories are devised without any acknowledgment of other subjugated beings suffering from humanity/the human.[6]

For example, I remember the first time I read a highly regarded paper that makes some claims about how our practices with animals and with one another direct and shape our notions of "human" and "animal."[7] Interestingly, the author focuses exclusively on ways in which we shape and subsequently teach these terms—*human* and *animal*—by our interactions with other humans (for the concept "human") and actual animals such as cows, pigs, sheep, dogs, and so on for the concept "animal."

I remember thinking what an extraordinary oversight or maybe a privilege it is to not also have to learn what "human" and "animal" mean by other kinds of practices that may have had *nothing* to do with actual animals but have to do with someone treating you terribly while calling you an animal. Or seeing members of your community being beaten or murdered because the cops considered them "nonhuman." Or constantly to realize that your people are never offered up as exemplars of "humanity" and have been considered not-quite-human for the past five hundred or so years.

Maybe when you are viewing these practices from a distance, you tend to not even think of them as being relevant to these terms, no matter how obviously relevant they might actually be. But I think if you experience it yourself, if you belong to an animalized group, if you're marked with a certain kind of social history and position, it's hard many times not to think of these terms—*human* and *animal*—with respect to something *other* than just species membership. They're not just metaphors. *They* really mean you're not one of them: you're not human. It's hard to think of these terms as being shaped only by how we interact with or use other species. It's hard not to see how *racial practices* have also shaped these words.[8]

Like the author of that paper, we tend to be blind to the fact that in both the narrative of speciesism and the narrative of racism the members of the losing side both fall short of *real* human status and, as a result, their suffering and their deaths are mundane, normal, and expected.

In my view of things, the "humanity" trumped up in one narrative is the same "humanity" trumped up in the other. If we want to make a connection, *this* is the connection we should be making. We're really not "comparing" anything in this type of thinking. We're noting a common source. The connection we make is not found *in* the oppressions themselves or the oppressed bodies. It's about realizing that we're wrong to focus on human bodies or animal bodies or what those bodies and souls face in being oppressed when we want to make "connections." All we need to do is focus on and make salient "the human" in both cases.[9]

As you see, taking a different entry point leads us to a different articulation and understanding of speciesism (*and racism*) and, with this different framework, we avoid the problems and useless debates that the standard framework generates. That's not to say the framework I've provided here as one example of something different will not encounter its own problems. But I am hoping it will also generate new questions, debates, and challenges, and clash with other frameworks to create ever fresher perspectives and even newer, differently informed frameworks.

Gloria Anzaldúa's guiding quote, with which I opened this chapter, indicates a way to keep the animal advocacy movement alive and healthy. Animal advocates can't be afraid to mix our ways of knowing, our consciousnesses, and our ways of experiencing the world. We should learn from each other even when we disagree. We shouldn't be afraid to theorize from our position and social location in the world—so long as we don't prevent others from doing so as well. We shouldn't be afraid we'd be penalized for deviating from what's expected . . . at least not in a movement like animal liberation, wherein so much hangs in the balance. And we shouldn't see these new ways of thinking as "infecting" the holy, existing standard order of knowledge. Most times, it's precisely by daring to break with the current logic that we can ever imagine anything new and truly for the better.[10]

15

Why Animal Liberation Requires an Epistemological Revolution

◆

Aph Ko
February 24, 2016

When you learn the language of the oppressor, you also inherit their worldview. As Frantz Fanon argues in Black Skin, White Masks, "A man [sic] who possesses a language possesses as an indirect consequence the world expressed and implied by this language."[1]

In most of our mainstream social justice movements, whenever activists across racial lines talk about "whiteness" they tend to do so only in terms of representation or leadership; however, very rarely do they speak about it in terms of the actual theory *they* use to structure their understanding of oppression.

Many activists speak of "decolonizing" themselves from the system without realizing that the basic building blocks they have used to structure their campaigns are actually products of the system they're trying to fight. We've inherited our conceptual tools and activist theories from the Eurocentric system. Before we can start "dismantling" this system of oppression, we first need to understand how we're still chained to it through the theory we employ to understand and discuss oppression.

In other words, liberation can't happen until we change the way we understand oppression.

In our mainstream animal rights movements, the dominant thought is: *Animal oppression is its own oppression and it has nothing to do with race or gender (or any other marker of difference).*

This is a line of thought I'm quite familiar with considering I constantly see tweets or receive messages from animal rights activists who are upset with the mission of Black Vegans Rock because they don't understand why we are talking about race and animal oppression at the same time.

The idea that oppressions manifest *separately* and then randomly "connect" at different points is *exactly* the problem I'm having with the animal rights movement and most other mainstream social justice movements. What's more, when activists who subscribe to Eurocentric thinking attempt to "connect" these issues or oppressions, they usually do so disingenuously. (Syl's chapter immediately preceding this one does a brilliant job breaking this down.)

Some activists share memes in which different, violated bodies are held up as examples of connecting oppressions, as though these bodies connect *because* of the *ways* their bodies are treated. In our movements, we have been organizing and theorizing around the *literal, physical* bodies of the oppressed, rather than going to the root of these oppressions *conceptually*. Most well-intentioned activists who use memes featuring a lynched black person and a lynched nonhuman animal are missing the point: What makes the physical violation of these bodies possible is their citizenship of the space of the Other or the "subhuman." They were all smuggled onto a hierarchy to bolster the superiority of the white ruling class.

Comparing and contrasting the literal/physical violations these subjects experience misses the conceptual boat since the reason why they are each oppressed is precisely because they are *all* citizens of the same subhuman space. Naturally, their oppressions might physically resemble one another since they have a common oppressor. But they are not being oppressed because they are "like" each other. There is nothing to compare. They are being oppressed because they have been labeled as less-than-human wherein *human* is defined as the superior and ideal white species. Our constant reflex to compare oppressions between victimized groups signals that we might need to develop a new grammar for talking about white human terrorism. To keep "comparing" these literal/physical oppressions to one another to show how they are the same is tautological.[2]

For example, saying, "Black people experience racism and, therefore, are treated *like* animals" is redundant because **racism is *already* entangled with speciesism.** What black folks are experiencing isn't "like" nonhuman animal oppression: it is a part *of* it. We are spending way too much time in our movements organizing around the physical oppressions of these bodies, which is problematic as we're not getting to the conceptual root of why these oppressions are happening in the first place. As activists, if we don't get to the root of oppressive behavior, then we risk reproducing the oppressive framework in our own liberation movements.

This result signifies that we are having a problem in our movements at the theoretical level.

A Eurocentric GPS

Imagine you get into a car and you have a GPS. When you type in the address you get a map, a representation of the territory you're in.

The issue we're having in our activist movements is that the map that's showing up on our activist GPS screen currently isn't matching the landscape we're on. This is because those in power have provided us with the map for liberation. Therefore, all of the oppressed are in traffic, honking at one another. We are all lost, trying to find the different roads the map keeps directing us to, which don't seem to exist on our terrain. The map isn't a real representation of what's before us. All it's doing is making us drive in circles, under the illusion that we are making progress on our trip.

In other words, the "intersections" the map tells us are there aren't real because the territory we're on has no intersections. We exist on one massive field labeled *subhuman*, where these systems are fused together and embedded within the soil of the terrain.

Our activist GPS is programmed with coordinates from the "human" terrain, which is why we can't get to our destination. The activist GPS we're using doesn't realize that these oppressions are fused together already. The goal for those of us who are minoritized is to spend time creating new maps. We need to orient ourselves toward the human–animal divide, rather than *only* our own specific physical oppression.

Some activists fail to realize how the maps they're using to guide them toward liberation are Eurocentric. My proof that this is so lies in the ways some activists try to analyze their *own* oppression without a meaningful analysis of animality. For example, *Everyday Feminism*, one of the largest digital magazines in the US devoted to intersectional feminist analysis, released a video by a feminist named Celia Edell. Edell argued that feminists aren't morally required to be vegan and they don't need to incorporate animal oppression into their feminist analyses.[3]

The video falls flat because veganism isn't just a diet, nor solely a means to politicize literal animal oppression. A lot of us aren't just talking about animal oppression, but animality, which is a Eurocentric construct that has contributed to the oppression of any group that deviates from ideal white homo sapiens. For many vegan feminists (myself included), the video was upsetting because when you actually understand the connections between oppressions in a non-Eurocentric context, you begin to realize how incorporating an analysis of animality into your activism strengthens your own frameworks.

In an article I wrote for the *F Bomb* titled "The Feminist Case for Veganism,"[4] I argued that, "When we adopt value systems from a white supremacist, patriarchal system, we jeopardize our liberation movements. We must always question scripts produced by the systems that oppress us and recognize that ending both messages falls under the same feminist agenda. Ultimately, feminists would do well to realize that the very bodies and topics that don't seem like they relate to their own oppression might be the very key to their liberation."

Eurocentric maps for liberation make it possible (ironically) for other popular feminists like Akilah Hughes, whom I talk about in chapter 2, to explain intersectionality to feminists using animal products as props in her viral video, "On Intersectionality in Feminism and Pizza."[5]

There's almost something tragic and comical about activists failing to realize the blatant missing piece to the activist puzzle: that your *own* oppression is anchored to your citizenship as a "subhuman" or "animal" in contemporary society. This is what makes racism, sexism, and all other "isms" possible. These "isms" are *expressions* of being labeled less-than-human. Therefore, this issue isn't just race-based or gender-based; it's *simultaneously* one of species as well.

If we're not organizing around this human–animal divide, then we aren't properly getting to the root of our oppression.

Within a Eurocentric analysis, activists have to spend all of their time "connecting" issues because everything is always and already singular and separate at the root. This should be our first sign that the theory we're using is designed around the experiences of the white elites, not our own.

When White People Become Racialized/Animalized

The massive domain of subhumans includes some white folks who fail to attain "ideal" homo sapiens status. We can look at the ways low-income white people in the US are racialized and framed through a subhuman narrative where "redneck" is used as a racial marker to distinguish between ideal white homo sapiens who are successful, wealthy, and "civilized," and low-income folks who are "naturally inferior" and beyond remediation.

TV shows like *Here Comes Honey Boo Boo* ride on "trailer-trash" aesthetics and "white trash" stereotypes in order to propel the narrative. *Here Comes Honey Boo Boo* is a reality show that follows six-year-old Alana and her family as their lives unfold in Georgia. Alana, known as Honey Boo Boo, is actually a child beauty pageant contestant who was initially discovered on the show *Toddlers and Tiaras*. In that show, her strange antics and "redneck"-style language during the confessionals entertained viewers, which is how she landed her own reality TV show. However, Alana portrays every stereotype of a southern redneck, from her slang/country speech to four-wheeling through mud. In an article on *Jezebel* called "Honey Boo Boo Struggles with Bodily Functions," the writer features a video from the show where Alana is sitting with Miss Georgia, who is depicted as the ideal white human subject.[6] Miss Georgia is tall, slim, well-mannered, and attractive. She is framed as the opposite of Alana. They sit in a bakery shop together eating cake and Miss Georgia offers her tips on etiquette.

Alana's character is juxtaposed with this white ideal woman to demonstrate how Alana is naturally inferior because of her class; she can't even *perform* ideal white femininity, so far is it removed from her natural character. Alana shoves cake into her mouth and expels gas on camera. The fact that Alana is so young bolsters the idea that her inferiority (due to her "low-class" status) is innate. She even uses "ratchet-style" language, suggesting that her class positions her "closer" to blackness than ideal whiteness. Her inability to restrain herself and perform as a proper white, human, feminine subject marks her as naturally inferior and inherently needing to be "tamed" and "controlled."[7]

The animalization of beings labeled or framed as "subhuman" suggests that "animal" is *itself* a racial opposite to the glorified white species. This means that "whiteness" signifies not only race and skin tone, but also an ideal way of *being*. "Animal" signifies a different type of racial citizenship that's *informed* by characteristics from those labeled "subhuman."

Exploring the Subhuman Territory
and Abandoning the Eurocentric Map

Let me reiterate: *Our mainstream social justice movements are doomed so long as Eurocentric theory is used to structure the logic of these movements.* (Yes, this means that even activists of color reproduce some of these issues in their campaigns.)

The fact that some folks are able to subtract race from the animal-oppression conversation is terrifying because, for so long, the mainstream animal advocacy movement has been throwing resources at efforts to "fix" the problem of cruelty toward animals without thoroughly examining what the actual problem is and how it's sustained. Animal rights organizations fund public campaigns to expose people to the cruelty of physical animal oppression (normally factory farming). The mainstream animal rights movement assumes that "adding" race back into the conversation means putting financial resources behind diversity initiatives. In the movement, race is only talked about in regard to including marginalized people in animal advocacy efforts; however, it's not talked about in a way that demonstrates how animals *themselves* are racialized. The further you stray from the *ideal* white homo sapiens imagination, the easier it is for you to be labeled "subhuman" or "animal."

The subtraction of race from the conversation is also chilling since oppressed people who are buying into Eurocentric logic are using that *same* logic to supposedly fight Eurocentric systems that are oppressing them. You can't create effective liberation movements if you don't completely understand the anatomy of your oppression.

In order for the oppressed (subhumans) to have a new citizenship that isn't inferior to those in power (glorified white humans), we need to have an epistemological revolution. This means that as conscientized black folks who reject Eurocentric logic, we have to fight, not just for vapid superficial representation in the mainstream animal liberation movement, but also for the right to produce knowledge, to create theory, and to rearticulate the way oppression actually manifests itself. Through this, animal liberation will be a by-product of our epistemological revolution.

16

How Social Media Serves as a Digital Defibrillator for "the American Dream"

◆

Aph Ko
November, 2016

In 2012, I fell in love with The Misadventures of Awkward Black Girl, a web series created by and starring Issa Rae. Rae was, for the most part, widely celebrated by mainstream black culture because of her quirky ways and her relatable storylines of social embarrassment. It was refreshing to watch a black woman use DIY aesthetics to entertain hundreds of thousands, especially in a mainstream white Hollywood culture that pretty much acted as if black people weren't even born yet. Rae even inspired me to make two indie web series of my own.

Rae's creativity catapulted her into the spotlight with over a million views of her YouTube channel. She garnered the attention of Pharrell Williams and even TV show impresario Shonda Rhimes. Rae has been listed on the Forbes "30 under 30" list twice, and she has been featured in magazines such as *Essence* and *Rolling Stone*. Her YouTube series has been turned into an HBO show called *Insecure* and she has even published a memoir!

The rise of Issa Rae and her subsequent success sounds more like an American-dream fairytale than just a standard "success" story. For me in particular, her achievement marked a significant moment for the millennial imagination where the American dream became repackaged: *white people were no longer the obvious gatekeepers to success; social media was.*

Rae's journey from being poor to being on the cover of *Essence* is sold to minoritized folks in a way that revives the narratives and politics of the American dream. A popular black digital space called *Madamenoire* featured a story about Rae's success as well.[1]

Rae's digital success story isn't unique. We can think of Numa Perrier and Dennis Dortch of Black&SexyTV, whose YouTube web series *The Couple* was picked up by HBO, and whose other web series, *Roomie Lover Friends,* was optioned by BET. The success of black stars like Rae and Perrier comes at a time when fifty percent of millennials believe the American dream is dead.[2] These millennials wouldn't be wrong, considering that "in the U.S., someone born in the lowest economic bracket has about a 8% chance of making it to the top."[3]

Just as black folks were beginning to bury the American dream, rightfully pointing to its racist, neoliberal foundation designed to perpetuate the disenfranchisement of minorities, innovators came in with their social media platforms, using them as digital defibrillators to revive it. They repackaged it and called it Facebook, YouTube, Twitter, Instagram, and Tumblr. It's not a coincidence that almost every single inventor of these platforms is a white man.

If you use YouTube, Instagram, Facebook, and Twitter, you too can make it to the top, which means visibility in a white mainstream marketplace. Fame and wealth are promised to young minorities who show a commitment to obsessively using and engaging with white social media platforms. In our hyper-engagement and distraction in the online world, it's easy to forget that once again white men are the gatekeepers of our success.

From Poverty to Hollow Fame: Technologized Sharecropping

Fame in the United States is presented as the perfect distraction *and* solution to systemic racism and poverty. Becoming famous is sold as something you have individual access to if you try hard enough. You can seemingly control your own image and get your own fans if you use the right technology. The right technology, of course, happens to be social media platforms that are created by those in the dominant class. Social media platforms have been framed as the tools that can close the representational gap between whites and blacks.

One of the shortfalls of representation rhetoric is that it advertises a simplistic blueprint for racial equality in which people of color are visually "included" in spaces regularly reserved for white people. The dominant thought is: *If we just show more minoritized faces in the white marketplace, then progress is being made.*

When fame and visibility are advertised as the only prerequisites for success, it appears as though *anyone*, regardless of race or socioeconomic status, can "make it" if she or he tries hard enough.

The idea of being plucked from poverty to be on the cover of a magazine is sold time and again as "progress," and social media provides a false sense of control over one's own destiny. Although more and more conscious people realize that the American dream is racist and unattainable, some don't seem to realize that it has merely been technologized, and our attempts at trying to "make it" through social media are merely an extension of that same dream.

Think about Tyra Banks from the TV show *America's Next Top Model*. She began scouring social media sites to cast models for the show. Instagram became her go-to space for finding faces that stood out. Eventually on the show, social media actually became a part of the models' scores, where viewers at home could vote for their favorite models, thereby providing them with the illusion that they were "part" of the show. In reality, they were just helping to strengthen the brand.

Although there are certainly many success stories that occur online, these send a message to disenfranchised youth who are sure to be exploited in their attempts to be recognized. You are rewarded for participating in the spectacle of social media in the hopes of becoming famous, as though fame alone will transport you to a new world where you will be admired and adored. Individual stories of social media success work to revive us during the days when we feel like there's no hope of ever "making it."

We can even think about pop star Rihanna casting Sanam, a woman of color, on Instagram in her music video, "Bitch Better Have My Money."[4] Rihanna found Sanam's photos on Instagram and started following her account. After featuring her in the music video, Sanam's visibility increased online. She was even featured in *Vogue* magazine.[5] Although this exposure offered an incredible opportunity for Sanam, the casting also marked a moment for people to revive their belief in social media as a vessel for success and elevation. This in turn served as a public-service announcement to those struggling to get visibility online: *keep laboring because a celebrity might be watching*. In fact, in an article on *Mashable* titled "Rihanna Found Her 'BBHMM' Henchwoman Thanks to Instagram," the author states, "Don't panic—but there's a possibility Rihanna may be creeping on your Instagram right now."[6]

The hyper-fixation on the self and the obsession with "making it" (not even for financial gain, but fame) has completely revolutionized the way the Internet functions. The demand for social media is fueled by disenfranchised people who really believe that clicks and hits will help them make it to the top, because an individual like Sanam was lucky enough to be lifted out of the crowd. This sentiment was echoed in an interview in *Vice* where Sanam states, "It's hard to make art when you're a woman, especially a woman of color, just because it's not respected in the same way as a white male artist's work. . . . Being in the video, I feel like that's given me a little bit more of a platform to talk about that kind of stuff."[7]

The main obstacle to creative folks seeking fame, however, is not that it is elusive but that the digital labor that some minoritized people employ isn't seen as labor, but free public material. They do the work; they contribute to the social media brand; they rarely see any real profit.

Facebook owns Instagram,[8] which means that Facebook can technically use all of the images you put on Instagram. That reality is an especially troubling phenomenon in the natural-hair world, where black women are encouraged to share hair tips, videos, and photos with each other through Instagram, yet their images are taken and used by exploitative natural-hair companies in their Facebook advertisements. I have personally encountered businesspeople who have attempted to sell hair-growth products for black women on Facebook, yet have used images of unrelated black women with long, natural hair on Instagram in their advertisements, without the latter's consent or knowledge. The companies end up financially profiting off the Instagram images, claiming there's nothing ethically wrong with this trend since they are giving the women in the images "exposure." Exposure becomes an exploitative form of social currency that we specifically allot to minorities.

It's a modernized version of sharecropping—a system of exploitation that followed the legal emancipation of black people in the United States. Some argue it was basically another way to keep black folks economically chained to white people under the guise that they were freely laboring:

> Sharecropping is a system where the landlord/planter allows a tenant to use the land in exchange for a share of the crop. This encouraged tenants to work to produce the biggest harvest that they could, and ensured they would remain tied to the land and unlikely to leave for other opportunities. . . . High interest rates, unpredictable harvests, and unscrupulous landlords and merchants often kept tenant farm families severely indebted, requiring the debt to be carried over until the next year or the next.[9]

Today, young poor folks are expected to labor on white digital platforms while having virtually no ownership over the material they create.

In an article on the *Fader* titled, "Black Teens Are Breaking the Internet and Seeing None of the Profits," Doreen St. Felix writes about the ways that young black people are creating new terms and concepts without remuneration. She tells the story of Kayla Newman, who coined the phrase "Eyebrows on Fleek," as well as twenty-year-old Denzel Harris, known as Meechie, who uploads his dancing videos to YouTube. After racking up thousands of subscribers, Meechie's channel was shut down by YouTube for copyright infringement. St. Felix writes:

> Part of the reason the originators of viral content are stripped from their labor is because they don't technically own their production. Twitter does, Vine does, Snapchat does, and the list goes on. Intangible things like slang and styles of dance are not considered valuable, except when they're produced by large entities willing and able to invest in trademarking them.[10]

The promise of success for black digital creators is compounded by the fact that they are playing on a digital playground designed by white men. What's worse, because large companies rarely invest in black entrepreneurs because of the implicit assumption that black people don't create groundbreaking technological ideas or that black people are financially irresponsible,[11] black folks are forced to rely on these social media platforms to generate any type of cashflow. Again, this need makes these creatives vulnerable to exploitation and even plagiarism.

Even successful black social media stars like Akilah Hughes experience co-optation of their work by larger white corporations. Recently, her YouTube comedy video titled, "How to Be an Introvert—According to Tumblr Ep. I," was repackaged without her consent for a *Buzzfeed* video called, "The Perfect Weekend for an Introvert." They chose a white woman to play the lead and allegedly stole the whole concept of the video from Hughes.[12] Popular black trans activist Kat Blaque writes:

> We could, of course, argue that everything is free game and that no one owns anything, but consider that in the almost two years Akilah's video has been posted, it's managed about 54k views and Buzzfeed's in the space of a day has managed 115k views. According to vidIQ, that estimates about $80 of total earnings over the space of about 2 years for Akilah's video and $172 for Buzzfeed's in the space of a day.[13]

Akilah's experience with Buzzfeed demonstrates how young creatives struggling to break into the industry are placed in a perennial cycle of exploitation because asymmetrical power relations are built into the architecture of digital work. This is why many mainstream organizations now require young applicants to submit five-to-ten creative ideas on their applications before they are even hired. I was once asked by a large white feminist magazine to apply for a position they were hiring for because they liked my work. Part of the application process included listing five article ideas for their magazine. After being told I wasn't hired, I saw one of my ideas published on the website a month later.

Mark Zuckerberg's Tools Will Never Dismantle White Supremacy

If *The Cosby Show* was the pinnacle of a notional post-racial culture wherein black folks who worked "hard enough" were promised a lucrative future and white normalcy, then the digital realm has picked up where it left off and is perpetuating a similar narrative: *You too can make it if you just try hard enough, regardless of your race or socioeconomic status.*

The discussion of systemic racism and sexism is largely thought of as a "real-world" problem, not a digital one. Social media creates the illusion of transcending your bodily limitations, where you can create a new online citizenship that isn't bound by systems of oppression. It offers an empty promise of success to minorities if they continue to participate and believe in the system. *You will be rewarded. If you're not making it on Facebook, well then . . . start an Instagram account. If that's not working, get a Twitter account. If that doesn't work, start a YouTube channel.* Just as Social Security numbers reflect your citizenship in a particular national space, listing the social media sites you have accounts with becomes a way to authenticate your citizenship online. Social media platforms become post-racial tools that anyone can use. The more you participate, the better your chances of climbing to the top. If you fail, or you don't reach your goals, it's because you didn't try hard enough!

This paradigm constantly requires you to work at being a better digital citizen, where your citizenship is determined and defined by white social media gatekeepers. People from lower socioeconomic backgrounds are sold the myth that sacrifice and perpetual struggle are patriotic acts that preserve the strength and uniqueness of America. They are told they are the anchors of the patriotic system and they shouldn't mind working for nothing because they might be at the top one day, too! Their hopes and dreams of getting out of poverty are transformed into a special type of fuel that keeps the engine of white social media platforms purring.

Even social justice activists are donning the logos of white social media platforms. In the iconic photo of Black Lives Matter activist DeRay Mckesson being arrested during a protest against the murder of Alton Sterling in Louisiana, Mckesson wears a shirt with the words #STAYWOKE, with a Twitter logo. The tech billionaire Marc Benioff tweeted, "Yes that is a @Twitter @blackbirds logo. Amazing to see tech as vehicle for social change." Benioff essentially highlighted Mckesson's arrest as a moment for diversity branding for Twitter.[14]

Social media has absolutely revolutionized activism in particular. As Kat Lazo, an indigenous Latinx feminist, argues in a talk called "Feminism Isn't Dead, It's Gone Viral," "The Internet has given us tools and platforms that previous feminists could have only dreamt of. . . . Online feminism is the future of feminism."[15] However, because the American dream has been technologized, even digital activists are being seduced by the spectacle of fame. This is, in part, why most activists have created YouTube channels where they talk into their cameras as though they are auditioning for their own television shows. They have almost "celebritized" themselves and turned their activism into a brand from which they can profit.

Digital activists who predominantly use YouTube and Facebook to create content to advance their brands have opened up markets for people like Chad Sahley, the CEO of Social Bluebook. Mimicking Kelley Blue Book, which values used and new vehicles to enable individual consumers to be better informed about their potential purchases, Social Bluebook is a new platform where activists and creators can find out their "worth" so they know what they should charge people who are interested in their services. In fact, the tagline for the website is KNOW YOUR WORTH. Creating social-justice content online has been transformed into a "transaction." On Social Bluebook, your social media reach and your engagement with social media platforms determine your worth. In fact, your worth as a digital citizen is determined by how many people "follow" you.

Determining one's worth and influence through social media is reminiscent of the annual Root 100 list. Every year, the *Root* (a popular black news website) puts out a list of a hundred influential African Americans. The staff at the *Root* determines your influence through your social media scores, which they measure through your influence, reach, substance, and Twitter-follower count. These are the units used to measure black folks' influence and worth. This scoring system conflates popularity with radicalism.

To a certain extent, the Internet *has* been life-changing for those of us who have used it purposefully to learn about activism and engage in critical thinking and movement building. I am definitely not one of those who'd state uncritically that the whole Internet is problematic, because it's not. I acknowledge that oppression and liberation are very messy spaces and that messiness needs to be honored. However, how has the actual structure of certain social media platforms anchored to "fans" and "followers" impacted the way activists are allowed to do work? What are the discursive repercussions of Black Lives Matter activists relying on social media platforms designed to perpetuate capitalist fantasies to dismantle white supremacy?

As someone who uses social media, I have found it to be a vital and efficient resource for reaching out to others and educating communities. However, the Internet is still largely governed by the same racist and sexist rules that structure the "real" world. One could even argue that the Internet gives white supremacy full access to black activists and their thoughts, which is perhaps one of the largest downsides of using the Internet to engage in racial justice work.

It's hardly a surprise that surveillance is an issue, as reports show that Black Lives Matter activists are being followed and watched at protests, and even online. A report on the *Intercept* stated that the Department of Homeland Security "collects information, including location data, on Black Lives Matter activities from public social media accounts, including on Facebook, Twitter, and Vine."[16] In October 2016, the ACLU announced that "Facebook, Twitter, and Instagram gave Chicago-based company Geofeedia access to user information that helped law enforcement agencies monitor and target activists of color."[17]

Audre Lorde famously noted, "The master's tools will never dismantle the master's house." One has to think, therefore: Is there a better way to engage in activist practices without using capitalistic social media platforms? Alternatively, is there a way to use these platforms while also disrupting them? Although these social media spaces have definitely helped some African Americans move from the margin to the center in regard to representation, is the center where we actually want to be when we can be commodified and plugged into a problematic system?

In her text *Feminist Theory: From Margin to Center*, bell hooks writes, "To be in the margin is to be a part of the whole but outside the main body."[18] For years, feminists have been assuming that the center is where liberation is located without realizing that the center might be disastrous for our movements. Even hooks notes this in a later essay:

> Though incomplete, these statements identify marginality as much more than a site of deprivation; in fact I was saying just the opposite, that it is also a site of radical possibility, a space of resistance. It was this marginality that I was naming as a central location for the production of a counter-hegemonic discourse that is not just found in words but in habits of being and the way one lives.[19]

Perhaps the revolutionary site has always been outside of the main body. Is it time for us to head back to the margins, but on our own terms, to revive the radical core of our projects? I mean, the fact that we want to dismantle white supremacy but many of us can't even imagine deleting our Facebook profiles and Twitter accounts suggests we might be more plugged in than we previously imagined.

I don't have the answers. But it's becoming increasingly obvious that social media is beginning to carry out the legacy of the American dream in insidious ways that both distract us through, and perpetuate the seductions of, white supremacist capitalism.

17

REVALUING THE HUMAN AS A WAY TO REVALUE THE ANIMAL

◆

Syl Ko
December, 2016

Introduction: How Do We Decolonize?

WE ARE ALL ANIMALS.

In this chapter, I'd like to examine this slogan in a way that demonstrates what one form of decolonial thinking looks like. I've mentioned in earlier chapters the need to decolonize our thinking in anti-racism and animal advocacy but it might not be clear what such a task entails. Many people register the call to "decolonize" in a very literal sense. From this point of view, an actual colonial event or encounter is the constitutive characteristic we think needs addressing in "decolonizing." In this sense, we take European settler–colonialism to have displaced beings from their original dwellings; ended or shredded important social ties and traditions; and restricted moral, legal, and social rules such that they advantage one group while disadvantaging and casting out "inferior" others as mere resources. The decolonial impulse in the context of animal advocacy, then, seeks to undo the narrative that the "natural world" is an entity detached from us and exists primarily as an object for our human needs and interests.

The aims of the animal liberation movement or animal advocacy in general seem consistent with the aims of a decolonizing impulse. Most animal advocates believe that by *including* animals in major, well-established models of morality, political theory, or the legal tradition, they *are* in the business of decolonizing. If colonial encounters intended to push animals and other nonhuman life to the sidelines and, in doing so, stripped them of their subjectivity and worth, then decolonizing this system will entail bringing animals and other nonhumans to the center and imbuing them with subjectivity and worth akin to human beings.

The same manifestation of this decolonial impulse can be seen in areas devoted to anti-racist activism. Most anti-racist advocates, regardless of race or ethnicity, believe that resisting the colonial narrative—in which people of color, particularly those who are indigenous and who are black, were excluded from social and intellectual spaces—is to *include* them in those spaces. Diversity initiatives are supposed to be *in themselves* decolonizing measures.

It, therefore, might come as a surprise when people like myself put forward work that seeks to "decolonize" how we think about animals and how we ought to think about ourselves and each other, especially as racialized beings. Aren't movements like anti-racism/civil rights and animal advocacy themselves the *result* of decolonial efforts?

The tension in the question exists in which *sense* we understand what it means to decolonize. As opposed to focusing on the literal colonial encounter and the implications this has had on how we think of all beings on the planet and the planet itself, some thinkers are calling us to focus on *coloniality*—the mindset and knowledge system that *preceded, accompanied,* and *made possible* colonial encounters. If we attend to coloniality rather than restricting our focus to literal colonial encounters, then merely including previously excluded beings in our models and frameworks serves to *reproduce* the conditions that created the original problems. Why? Because, on the surface, what seems to be an alternative stipulation is, in fact, a suggestion provided *by* the existing framework or model—the one we are supposed to be resisting. If we use the existing framework or model—the established *mindset*—to articulate a "solution" to a problem that that model sustains, in what way are we "dismantling"?

Nelson Maldonado-Torres, who is a specialist in decolonial thinking and extensively studies, and who writes about and thinks through the works of Frantz Fanon, recently argued against the popular "inclusion" approach. He is discussing the neglect of work by people of color and the crisis regarding "illegal" immigration, but I think that what he says broadly applies to animals and other members of the environment as well:

> Universities cannot become real sanctuaries for people of color as long as what they consider sanctum continues to be premised on our secondary status, if not the expectation of our disappearance and the mere "inclusion" of our scholarship in the very same fields and structures that have denied those issues entry for so long. We will not go far if we fail to confront the reality that the liberal arts and sciences, themselves, not neo-fascist ideologues, are responsible for all of this. Likewise, our efforts to address and counter the racist forces that are becoming so obvious today—but that have been dominant all along—will be undercut if calls for increasing the number of sanctuaries for the undocumented collapse into the affirmation of discourses and practices of inclusion, instead of becoming part of the struggle for decolonization. The opposite of exclusion, in contexts structured by coloniality, is not inclusion, but decolonization. Inclusion, in these contexts, is just another form of coloniality.[1]

In the remainder of this chapter, I will attempt to show how the slogan WE ARE ALL ANIMALS succumbs to the sort of inclusive thinking that Maldonado-Torres refers to as "just another form of coloniality." Since I don't want this chapter to be too long, it will be necessary to gloss over a few details. Nonetheless, the point of this exercise is to demonstrate how one might look at a seeming innocuous statement or belief, extract and analyze components that tie it to a larger, problematic way of thinking, and then undo/redo it by thinking from an outside point of departure.[2]

Starting Assumption

For me, the easiest way to approach the slogan initially is to assume, first of all, that what is meant by WE ARE ALL ANIMALS is something innocent and intuitive: that we all belong to the same group despite the superficial distinctions that divide us into different *kinds* of that group. By virtue of belonging to the same kind, we should care about one another's interests. A more compelling way to frame this is as a basic reminder that we share the animal body and the animal condition with members of species other than homo sapiens. The reminder functions as a way to bring us closer and make us feel pity and love for other animals.

It's not entirely clear to me that this latter observation is intuitive. There are many instances in which the drive to relate to or pity another being is licensed by a perceived group-link or significant similarity. (I think perceiving a group-link is a different matter from perceiving a similarity, but I'll leave that thought as is.) Indeed, there are an equal number of instances in which a drive to exploit or harm a being gains its purchase through a perceived group-link or significant similarity as well. One might develop deep fondness for a primate after spending some time with her because of the wealth of shared similarities that ground our membership in the group "primate." However, that wealth of similarities also motivates us to valorize experimentation on primates. On the one hand, the nonhuman primates can make good animal friends, in relationships that benefit us both. On the other, they can make good subjects for scientific and anthropological inquiries that benefit only us and intrude upon their bodies and lives.

WE ARE ALL ANIMALS operates on the assumption that objective facts about similarities or differences substantively inform how we think morally. As illustrated in the case concerning primates, that's just not true. Similarities, differences, and ideas that revolve around group membership are not ahistorical or noncontextual. Similarities can certainly operate in favor of protecting and caring for another's interests. But that similarity has to be filtered through something else, some sort of rule, that instructs us to interpret said similarity as a reason to protect and care. If we apply a different rule to the same similarity, the complete opposite attitude and behavior is to be expected: the similarity is a reason to exploit and violate.

One simple example can be applied to the recognition of our shared animal body and animal condition, which—as I mentioned already—grounds the slogan. Those on the other side of the debate who defend using animals for our interests recognize our shared animal body and animal condition in the identical slogan. Their argument is something like: *If it is OK for animals to eat and use other animals and we are simply animals, then it should be OK for us to eat and use other animals, too.* So, as you can see, it can run in both directions.[3]

When we present objective matters of fact—like certain or all animals being similar to us or different from us in varying ways—those matters of fact are impotent until we filter them through human-made categories and concepts, which will govern how those facts should be interpreted.

The thinking exhibited in the slogan WE ARE ALL ANIMALS also questionably assumes that beings have to belong to one rational space in order for all of those beings to be considered "fit" members of our moral community. It never occurs to us that instead of rebelling against the established human–animal contrast by "doing the opposite"—pulling humans and animals into the same space—a better rebellion might consist of forming an utterly new basis by which we draw contrasts altogether. But more on that later.

The Slogan as a Response to Speciesism

I think there is a better way to explain WE ARE ALL ANIMALS that involves a larger debate on who is and who is not inherently morally worthy. Construed in this way, the slogan is an attempt to respond to *humanism*, or the tendency to hold members of the species homo sapiens as the definitive representation of value itself. That is, just being human is reason enough to be thought of and treated with dignity and respect.

An easy way to outline the difference between the mindset displayed in the slogan and the one displayed in conventional thinking is as follows:

(1) <u>All</u> *humans* are *animals.* [Inclusive]
(2) <u>No</u> *humans* are *animals.* [Exclusive]

While defenders of (2) agree that human beings obviously belong to the animal kingdom, they believe that the species line is morally significant. That is, whereas we might be animals *biologically,* we are different and special beings *ontologically.* One of the clinchers introduced by colonial thinking is that we are not just different and special when measured against all of the other animals, but we are their *opposite.* We ordinarily refer to this decisive separation as the human–animal binary, but I like to spell it out as humanity and animality being *contrasts* or *opposites* to make plain why the idea is so dangerous, especially for animals. If the human is the definitive representation of value itself, then, following the golden rule of the human–animal opposition, the animal is the definitive representation of the *absence* of value itself. That's not to say that we can't value animals. It's just to say that *if* animals are to be given any value, it's because they are of some value *to us.*

It goes without saying that those on the side of animals are usually disenchanted with the idea of humans or humanity being "special." They believe that animals are on the moral sidelines or even exterior to morality because of myths constructed to elevate humans and human capacities as central and innately valuable. Partly owing to this myth, we now believe we are justified in using/abusing animals however we wish, since they do not belong to our privileged group.

If I were to use my being human as a reason for why I should or should not be treated a certain way, there is even a term such people would wield against me: I am *speciesist.* This term is not merely intended to explain animal use and abuse as humans preferring their interests over and against animals' interests. This term is also (and especially) designed to illuminate what makes that preference for our own species *unjust.* Peter Singer, who popularized thinking about animal oppression in terms of speciesism, has this to say:

Just as a person's race is in itself nearly always irrelevant to the question of how that person should be treated, so a being's species is in itself nearly always irrelevant. If we are prepared to discriminate against a being simply because it is not a member of our own species, although it has capacities equal or superior to those of a member of our own species, how can we object to the racist discriminating against those who are not of his own race, although they have capacities equal or superior to those of members of his own race?[4]

Succinctly put, according to Singer an individual's species membership just shouldn't play a role in how we treat that individual if s(he) is sentient and the situation involves creating or preventing pain/suffering. If s(he) can suffer, then whether s(he) belongs to our species or not is irrelevant when it comes to how we ought to treat her/him. So, if it is wrong to, say, stamp on my foot because it hurts me, then it should also be wrong to stamp on a chimp's foot if that were to hurt him or her as well. That I am a human being and s(he) is a chimp is irrelevant to the matter if we both suffer from the same action. To think otherwise is to basically admit to one's speciesism.

Singer's view is very nuanced and he has many works clarifying his thesis, but I'm not interested in going into a philosophical exposition here. The main point is that animal advocates are very influenced by how Singer presents the case for speciesism and are now convinced that moral thinking along the lines of species is relevantly like racism and sexism. It is *bad*. And so they conclude from this that the only way to elevate the moral status of animals is to secularize or deglamorize being human.

This fills out the story about the slogan a little better and more charitably. The slogan is one way animal advocates secularize the human species: it brings to our attention that the human is just another kind of animal. They are trying to move us from (2) to (1). They believe that deglamorizing the human "down to" just its biological reality—a member of the animal kingdom—will perform the *emotional work* of creating a bond with other animals. We are just like them. We all belong to the same group. So, their interests should matter to us as much as *our* interests matter to us. I believe this might be what activists are getting at when they proclaim, "We are *all* animals." The end result is supposed to be a pull to include animals as serious members of our moral universe.[5]

As much as I understand the intention behind this kind of thinking, it has always revealed to me an emotional crisis among animal defenders. They advocate for the *heightening* of emotions when it comes to the similarities we share with animals by virtue of our capacity to experience suffering, while they advocate for the *cooling* of emotions when it comes to the bond we hold with our own species by virtue of even *more intense and relevant experiences and capacities.* On the one hand they claim there is something wrong with caring about human interests merely because we are all the same kind. After all, isn't that, in principle, like racism and sexism? But on the other hand they want to claim we should care about animal interests because . . . we are all the same kind. Thus, by their wish to lessen the importance of our human bond, they effectively neutralize the basis by which we would establish an emotional bond with other animals.[6]

Aside from there being an emotional crisis, though, the push for deglamorizing the human for the sake of elevating the animal also reveals to me a crisis in principles. To me, the following ways of thinking are two sides of the same coin:

Side #1: Elevating the human effectively deflates the animal.
Side #2: Deflating the human effectively elevates the animal.

Simply moving to the underside of a position is in no way revolutionary. It is an "opposite" position only insofar as an image reflected in the mirror is "opposite." As we all know, such an opposition is superficial and requires the original to sustain its existence. By moving to the "opposite" side, we do not destroy a way of thinking. It is a way we keep certain patterns of thinking *intact.* I think this is what Maldonado-Torres was getting at in his critique of inclusive measures.

If we adhere to there being something inherently contrary between "human" and "animal," then, yes, any attempt to sanctify humans and humanity will work against the interests of animals in general. And, by the same lights, if we want to make equal and so effectively "lift" animals to a rights-bearing level, we will have to desanctify being human. But to insist on this is to reveal that one actually *abides by the human–animal binary*. If we were really thinking outside of the binary, then there should be no issue in holding that human beings are a special kind and being human can operate as *a* reason to treat each other according to a standard. Outside of the binary, such thinking would not thereby negate profound obligations and duties to nonhuman members who share our world. There is no either/or relation. For a simple example, consider another distinction we draw that carries with it moral implications: family versus non–family members. That Aph is my sister gives me a reason to privilege her interests over those of the random person walking down the street. However, that does not mean that I do not have to consider the interests of the random person nor can I absolve my duties to him or her only on the grounds that s(he) is not my family member. Family members and non–family members do not qualify as terms of a binary, so I am able to privilege one without taking away from the very real obligations I owe the other. So, even if it is true that, biologically, we are all animals, this cannot be our rallying cry because, for it to do the work we want it to, we must remain trapped within the binary. We certainly don't want to do that: the binary is the reason why animals are in this position in the first place.

Freeing the Terms of the Binary

The flawed way of thinking as explored in the preceding section creates the impression that strong pro-animal positions (especially those that entail a vegan imperative) will always reach an impasse with oppressed groups fighting for their "humanity" that use the fact that they are human as grounds for their protest.

The move toward human liberation—or so the assumption goes in human-rights spaces—relies on *creating* and *strengthening* a human bond, *contra* Singer. To argue that we ought to *loosen* this tie is to miss the point that this tie has never been achieved, which is why we continue to witness gross violations of human rights. As a person who truly wants to see a world in which animals are not commodities and are free to live lives outside of human interests, I think these activists are onto something, even if I don't quite agree with the terms of their position. After all, if we cannot accomplish a deep tie among those who share *so many* similarities—biological and otherwise—*within* our own species, what hope is there for us to forge a deep emotional tie on the same grounds with beings who are much *less* similar to us?

As interesting as the implications are from this perspective, though, I'm not prepared to defend a special investment in humanity/other humans just because of fundamental similarities that we share. I already discussed earlier why dwelling on similarities doesn't in itself generate moral feelings or a morally significant bond.

Instead, I'd like to challenge the presumably unbreachable impasse by turning to the anti-/decolonial tradition critical of the category through which we think "the human." I believe that our obsession with (1)—the idea that "we are all animals"—has obscured one very obvious route for building an animal ethic. It has prevented activists from gleaning that anti-/decolonial efforts to rescue our notion of "the human" from its colonial grip is a project to liberate human beings *from the human–animal opposition*. In doing so, I think we have a nice (and creative) conceptual model to free *animals* as well.

To make sense of how this will work, let's briefly recall the inclusive and exclusive approaches:

(1) <u>All</u> *humans* are *animals*. [Inclusive]
(2) <u>No</u> *humans* are *animals*. [Exclusive]

And now let's introduce the third, or what I'll refer to as the decolonial approach:

(3) <u>Some</u> *humans* are *animals*. [Decolonial]

I will not discuss (3) at length here since the majority of my chapters have already investigated the *social* rendering of the notions "human" and "animal." As a recap, however, it is enough to say that whether or not a being is classified as "human" is morally relevant in cases where disparate treatment occurs between members of the species homo sapiens exclusively, not just in cases that involve members of the species homo sapiens and other species. The approach I'm proposing is to shift our understanding of animal oppression away from (2) and toward (3). Animals are inferior or nonexistent members of our moral imagination for the same reason that many humans are: they are not "human," understood in the *social* sense. They are all animals *socially* construed.

The anti-/decolonial tradition on which I draw is that which follows the work of Frantz Fanon and the Latin American writers influenced by sociologist Anibal Quijano. Even though these thinkers did not have nonhumans specifically in mind, their views bring major import and relevance to the question of the animal by virtue of their relevance to the question of the human. Through the work of this tradition, racial minorities fighting for their humanity present a challenge to the status quo rather than hope for conformity with it. They are not asking to be *included* in the idea of humanity that animal advocates want to make obsolete. They are undoing humanity as we know it. When oppressed groups, then, make claims to their humanity, something absolutely radical takes place.

Professor Zakiyyah Jackson suggests the claims to humanity "resignify and revalue humanity such that it breaks with the imperialist ontology and metaphysical essentialism of Enlightenment man." After raising the common assumption that oppressed groups cling to their humanity since they cannot dispose of something they do not possess, she challenges this assumption in her examination of scholars of race during the 1990s:

It is not that [racialized] critics [of posthumanism] simply sought admission into the normative category of "the human"; rather, they attempted to transform the category from within. . . . The hope was not that black people would gain admittance into the fraternity of Man—the aim was to displace the order of Man altogether. Thus, what they aspired to achieve was not the extension of *liberal* humanism to those enslaved and colonized, but rather a transformation within humanism.[7]

Members of oppressed groups are not *correcting* or *redefining* humanity but are literally changing the conversation around humanity altogether. Since the human–animal opposition gives meaning to the colonial rendering of both "human" and "animal," the challenge to humanity is a challenge to the binary.

To challenge *this particular* notion of humanity is not to *eliminate* all possible notions of humanity. Just because the European construal of what humanity ought to look like and designate doesn't work would not mean we should throw our hands up as if to say, *Well, all we can do now is avoid that concept altogether.* Just because a celebration of *that construal* of humanity leads to destruction everywhere does not mean *all* celebration of *any* construal of humanity will lead to the same results. Such a submission is again a lapse into colonial thinking—the idea that what governing groups in Eurocentric societies propose exhausts all ways of thinking. The anti-/decolonial tradition shows us that to save humanity and the planet we must re-enchant humanity.

Though many activists, scholars, and writers who are also animal advocates are excited about the work to oppose our current racialized, gendered, and able-bodied idea of the human/human being, they shy away from the conclusion that all of these views in my opinion point to: that the human needs to be "revalued and resignified." I believe they are afraid of this conclusion because they read these works through an orthodox lens. When Fanon or Sylvia Wynter proclaim the importance and centrality of humankind, and argue that the attempt to naturalize the human as a mere biological being, simply another animal, is *itself* a colonial project, they are leveling *part* of the racial critique at the Eurocentric creation of "the human" and—as I hold—"the animal" as well. To divorce these ideas from one another is to misunderstand the theoretical foundation these thinkers offer.[8]

Conclusion

I've tried to give a glimpse of what decolonizing work looks like by considering a popular slogan in the animal movement. Really, the gist of everything I have been saying is that decolonizing work is more than just attending to the literal ways in which certain beings have been excluded from moral, social, political, and legal domains. Decolonizing work is fundamentally about removing the threads that hold together narratives that underpin those domains. Coloniality is dangerous beyond its power to objectify, harm, and destroy living beings. Its poison lies in its monopoly over human consciousness. It tricks us into believing that wherever is the opposite of what currently exists is the "radical" or "revolutionary" place to land. But, again, these spaces are given to us *by* coloniality. We remain within the narrative it constructed. This is how we remain stuck in its snares.

Now back to animals.

What I have written in this chapter is both unremarkable and perhaps quite remarkable: the way to animal liberation partially requires us to free our notion of "the animal" from the binary (anything else is to repeat binary thinking). It's a stepping-stone to animals existing as beings for themselves. We should continue attending to their material conditions, of course. I just mean the project of physically liberating the animal has to go hand in hand with the work of freeing them from the binary *in our heads*.

Describing their struggle in *social* terms and recognizing that we have only really seen animals through this specific social veneer brings us to another remarkable point: we may have never really *thought* about animals— whether to what extent they are our moral conspecifics, or who they are in general. We have only thought about them in this literal, "biological," matter-of-fact way under the impression that this will give us clues or even answers about our obligations to them. In fact, their situation and who they are is tied to the larger, grander narrative that establishes who is human and innately valuable and who is not—a story that is *not* and never *has been* based on biology or biological facts. What will their situation be and *who* will they be when we find the courage to transcend the West's monopoly on storytelling and begin to tell a new story about and for ourselves?

18

Black Veganism Revisited

◆

Syl Ko
December, 2016

I initially felt uncomfortable when I referred to Aph's and my work as "black veganism." The discomfort stemmed mostly from the second word, because my relationship with that movement oscillates. I think most of us can feel in the pit of our stomach that there is something off and perhaps even wrong with the way we treat and use animals, especially animals used for consumption, experimentation, and entertainment. I think this is true regardless of whether we've said it out loud to others or even to ourselves. On the other hand, almost anything concrete that emerges from the animal advocacy movement has always seemed—to me, at least—a little embarrassing and not well thought out. The question of what our obligations are (if any) to animals, as well as to other nonhuman members of the planet, is a very difficult one. Throwing around facts about similarities between species or vacuous appeals to compassion does not seem to capture what this question is asking. It is an enormous question, and anyone who claims to have an easy answer is not doing the question justice.

For several reasons, inviting the label *black* to join the word *veganism* also contributed to this feeling of discomfort. First, I was afraid that the combination would be dismissed as black people merely participating in the vegan lifestyle and movement as we currently know it. That's certainly not what I mean by "black veganism." I was trying to get across the idea that black veganism is *internal* to the project of black liberation. The mainstream vegan lifestyle and movement is not designed to attend to our struggles as people of color, so I am not sure how simply participating in those spaces, as wonderful as that might be, liberates us from the racial logic that shapes how we feel about and view ourselves. A veganism generated from a different mindset should radically depart from whatever our ordinary notion of vegan ideology is, especially if we remember that defenders of mainstream vegan ideology are *still* struggling to come up with a suitable way to make the animal situation relevant to human oppressions. Black veganism faces no such task: the ideology in which the animal situation is articulated is embedded in black liberation ideology. There is no gap to bridge.

Secondly, I did not want to encourage anyone to participate in the liberal obsession with individuating groups when it comes to oppression, especially the demarcation of them using colonially derived categories such as racial labels or nation-states. This is not about *this* group doing veganism "their" way and *that* group doing veganism "their" way. It is fine for others to group themselves however they like and reveal how this might affect their vegan praxis. Again, that is not what I meant to accomplish with black veganism. Racism is simultaneously anti-*black* and anti-*animal*, as seen by racial ideology's elevation and celebration of "the human" and "humanity" particularly as Western and *white*. That simple fact escapes us in both the vegan and anti-racist movements. So, the consciousnesses that are fragmented in response to anti-black racism are the consciousnesses into which I am hoping to tap in order to redescribe and form a new narrative around the situation animals face.

Eventually, I put aside any reservations on both fronts by considering the overall value that could come about with this peculiar label. Merging *vegan* with *black* dissuades one from buying into the myth that the animal issue is a stand-alone one or can be understood or addressed by considering animal use/abuse and the usual rhetoric of suffering and compassion. As the vegan movement currently exists, the conventional approach is one in which most people restrict their focus to the material or *physical* conditions of nonhuman animals. There is little to no focus on coloniality and the concepts *it* provides, which ensure there will *always* be an "animal problem."

Such is the case whether we are abolitionists or welfarists or rationalists or see the issue as environmental as opposed to ethical or specifically ecofeminist or Afrocentric, or whatever tradition you espouse. So long as we continue to overlook the *colonial* dimension of this problem, we continue to undermine our own efforts. By "colonial dimension," I am not referring to the literal colonization of nonhuman animals insofar as we have taken over their bodies or have removed them from their lands and restricted them to certain spaces in line with our needs and interests. What I have in mind are the concepts that sustain coloniality and which are responsible for ranking not just human beings but every being on the planet.

As mentioned before, I also think merging *black* with *veganism* hints at the fact that reevaluating our ideas about nonhuman animals is an essential ingredient in the project of black liberation. One consequence of this gesture is that we have to also reevaluate our idea about what race and *racism* are and, subsequently, what black liberation looks like. Our ordinary ideas about race and racism might make it unclear as to how nonhuman animals and our attitude toward them have any connection to black liberation, or any other human liberation, for that matter.

The ordinary way we think and talk about race/racism places the accent on external modes of abuse, control, and inhibition: that is, an individual or groups of people—usually from the dominant racial group, but not always—are depicted as physically or *outwardly* acting on or directing their attitudes toward racial minorities. Lynching, slavery, police violence, racial slurs, denying someone a job, or restricting other opportunities based on race and the like are some common examples of what most likely come to mind when people think about racism. Now we are slowly acquainting ourselves with less-obvious forms of this external mode as demonstrated by protests aimed at the state of mainstream media or the ire directed at whom you choose to be with in an intimate relationship.

I think this popular (and sometimes singular) representation of racism as existing in the immediate foreground—as something observable, obviously bad, or evil, or something that affects *this* or *that* group— neutralizes our efforts to show just how deeply entrenched racial ideology is. That foregrounding also obscures just how much racial ideology plays a role in *most* oppressions, whether we explicitly recognize those oppressions as racial in nature or not.

We seem to be confusing the *spectacle* of race/racism for race/racism *itself*.[1] The machinery of racial logic directs our attention away from itself and toward some event or occurrence (a tragedy here or there, a protest today or tomorrow), while it keeps itself well hidden in the background, enabling it to disappear through its very effects.

When I suggest that reevaluating the animal must be internal to the project of black liberation, I don't have this external mode of racism in mind. Instead, I am referring to internal racism.

Internal racism is that painful and ever-present mode living inside every racialized minority. It's the feeling that we are not quite human. The anatomy of internal racism is quite complicated but it ought not be confused with the psychological effects of external modes of racism. In the latter case, the feeling is "we are not *treated like we are human,*" with the accompanying acknowledgment that we *are* in fact human. "Human" here, then, is still in terms of the physical. We *are* members of the species homo sapiens. With internal racism, however, there is a shift: the feeling is "we are *not* human" or "we are *sub*human" or, if we are having an especially honest moment, "basically, we are *animals.*" Now, the terms are social.

Internal racism is the result of affected individuals perpetuating their oppression by means of directing harmful racial ideas toward themselves. It comes about by "breathing in the same air," so to speak, as those who are privileged and internalizing the intellectual and aesthetic values, concepts, and so on that were designed from the viewpoint of the governing group and for the purpose and aims of maintaining that governance. Manifestations of this mode of racism are harder to observe. They come in the form of self-hatred, rage, embarrassment, and rejection of one's sub-"cultures";

a slavelike approval and endorsement/protection of the governing group's values, even though they were designed with racial exclusion in mind; a fear of producing radically new knowledge that is not in line with the status quo; and the constant feeling of inferiority, just to name a few.

In a world governed by racism, it should come as no surprise that internal racism, which is experienced only by racialized minorities, is generally neglected or minimized in ordinary analyses or venues. It should come as no surprise that people of color themselves also tend to focus overwhelmingly on external modes of racism above internal modes, given that we learn to think in accordance with what is conventional as soon as we enter the classroom or turn on the television. Although some important writers and artists of color stress the significance of internal racism—I'm thinking of people such as Steve Biko, Frantz Fanon, Sylvia Wynter, Carter Woodson—and aim to direct people of color toward this internal mode as the proper entry point for thinking and talking about racism, that process still has not caught on in the mainstream.

In almost all of my contributions to Aph's work, my argument is premised on thinking through the animal question as a confrontation experienced in internal racism. Black veganism is the consciousness that emerges from this confrontation. It is in this consciousness that we face the limit of blackness and perceive its entanglement with "the animal." And it is in this consciousness that we finally apprehend "the animal" as a vast social body. Thus, when we say that "basically, we are animals," we *feel* what it means for racial ideology to implement the colonial concept of "the animal" in order to bring destruction to beings all over the planet, human and otherwise. Our *feeling* is an epistemic resource. In black veganism, we learn to trust that feeling and use it as a launching pad to theorize how the colonial tool of animality affects *animals*. The discovery is monumental: animals did not inform our notion of "animality." "Animality" informed our notions of animals.[2]

So, what is black veganism and who is it *for*?

Let me answer in reverse order. Black veganism is not designed for black people only. After all, when we say we are anti-racism, whoever we are, I would hope that that means we are for black liberation. Otherwise, I don't know what being anti-racist means. Black veganism is simply *black* in its perspective. To illuminate this point, I'd like to borrow an example used by decolonial writer Walter Mignolo:

> A lake looks different when you are sailing on it than when you are looking at it from the top of the mountains surrounding it. Different perspectives . . . are not only a question of the eyes, then, but also of *consciousness* and of physical location and power differential—those who look from the peak of the mountain see the horizon and the lake, while those inhabiting the lake see the water, the fish and the waves surrounded by mountains.[3]

To remain within the terms of the example, lifelong boat-dwellers who learn about a mountain-dweller's perspective of the lake might have a very interesting conversation about the sorts of things that are overlooked by those people who have never seen the water up close, or the fish inhabiting the water and the ripples congregating at the shoreline. It is not that they are challenging the mountain-dwelling perspective or find that it is in error. Rather, as Mignolo puts it, it is a completely different logic. Mountain-dwellers can have a fuller picture of the world, and particularly the lake, if they trust that a different perspective can help them think about the world differently, even if it is a perspective they have never experienced.

Notice that this is not an essentialist claim (not that I am bothered by such a charge). Imagine how silly it would be to say that the boat-dweller endorses essentialism just because she or he is aware of having a different perspective of the lake from the mountain-dweller!

And finally, to answer the question: What *is* black veganism?

Black veganism is not a movement. It is not a statement, nor does it provide definitive answers to the hard questions about what our duties to nonhuman members of the planet are. We do not provide a substantive plan for dismantling coloniality. They are huge questions and I don't want to make light of them. We do not yet have the creative resources to provide many of these answers. Part of coloniality's task is to ensure that certain futures remain unimagined, that certain ideas remain unthinkable so that it seems that whatever we have now is all we have to work with.[4] Simply put, black veganism is a *methodological tool* to reactivate our imaginations. It is designed to relocate the animal question to a new and fresh space to find new and fresh answers as well as to benefit *any* oppressed being. From this fresh vantage point, any serious dismantling work will have to go farther than just how we view and treat one another. Dismantling racism will also require us to reconsider how we view and treat all life.

→ 19 ←

Creating New Conceptual Architecture

On Afrofuturism, Animality, and Unlearning/Rewriting Ourselves

◆

Aph Ko
December, 2016

It's a difficult task persuading marginalized folks that most of our mainstream movements to overturn systems of domination are structured through Eurocentric logic. In regard to racism, if you're not talking about police brutality, diversity in Hollywood, colorism,[1] or any other topic that can be captured on camera, then you're seen as irrelevant or a distraction from the goals of anti-racism. As a culture, we operate on the false idea that if you have a particular shade or tone of skin, that shade is supposed to reflect the state of your consciousness. This means that if you're black, your movements and efforts for liberation are automatically seen as de-centering whiteness; if you're white, you're seen as automatically racist and possessing privileges that you can never see or change. Despite our great intentions, a lot of us haven't realized that the ideological tools we use to create our anti-racist movements are already problematic.

When you're oppressed, the dominant class provides you with a map of the world. They decide what goes where, and who is or is not important. If as a black radical movement we're going to question our racial inferiority, we must also question the entire setup if we want real liberation: we cannot work within it. We have to question all "norms" produced out of the system we're trying to bring down, such as consuming animal flesh or possessing negative attitudes toward certain marginalized groups. What's necessary in order to decolonize (from) the system is to unlearn myths about our own bodies as well as all other bodies that are provided with "inferior" citizenships; that's because our inferiority is fictional. To only make yourself equal to the white man as your sole means of liberation isn't liberation: it's merely a restructuring of the white imagination, which is what has happened in our anti-racist movements today.

In particular, our automatic acceptance of a hierarchy that places white folks on top and animals at the bottom demonstrates how we are being bamboozled into accepting a system that ironically subjugates us as well due to our racial location in the hierarchy. Perhaps it hasn't occurred to us as black people that assuming animals are disposable is actually a product of being colonized by white supremacist patriarchy.

I would argue that there are concerted efforts never to get black people to develop these new relationships with animals or to have these conversations about animality and race. Black and brown people are specifically being targeted by meat-centric organizations[2] to construct a bond with their products, not only to ensure that black folks remain lifelong consumers of their products, but also so that black folks don't ever form a new relationship with animals outside of consuming their corpses. It's not in the interest of white supremacy to have black folks advocating for a type of racial liberation that points to the ways that animality has been employed as a racialized weapon of the dominant class.

We can easily think of McDonald's as an example of this. The company has an initiative called 365Black (it's a real website) in which they celebrate the black community and black culture every day of the year. Their tagline is DEEPLY ROOTED IN THE COMMUNITY. They put on gospel tours, give out scholarships to historically black colleges and universities, and tie themselves to black magazines like *Essence*. (Every time I go on their website, a McDonald's video ad pops up with a black family.) They even sponsor black bloggers who have a huge influence on thought in the black community. They put on an annual 365Black awards show, where they award black celebrities and change makers. In fact, in September 2015 director Ava DuVernay won a 365Black award for her film *Selma*.[3]

McDonald's forges a form of trust in communities that have felt let down by the mainstream US, economically, financially, and racially. The company has planted roots in black and brown communities, demonstrating they can single-handedly provide food and jobs for people living in them. In fact, my first job at the age of fourteen was at a McDonald's; so I understand personally why people are nostalgic for companies like this. The job was the first time that I ever felt independent, and I remember how proud I was when I could contribute money to the family bank account. To this day, if I smell fast food, it immediately evokes memories of my childhood and the first time I started working.

Many black vegans or food-justice activists tend to take McDonald's to task because they are advertising meat, and the conversation normally turns to the ways that meat has been detrimental to our health. However, we also have to realize how we've simultaneously adopted detrimental conceptual frameworks to define our own blackness, which is just as problematic and dangerous as consuming the products, not only because it's ruining our health and killing nonhuman animals, but also because it naturalizes a racist, speciesist hierarchy and value system that sustains white supremacy.

There's a real reason why so much effort is put into ensuring that black people subscribe to a particular *type* of blackness that's anchored to consuming animal products. Almost everything we know about our communities and ourselves is manufactured by white supremacy and yet we celebrate it, advertise it, and defend it as though it's our own. Corporate spaces and mainstream black blog sites pump out the same types of narratives about blackness because they are invested in making a profit, not in critical thinking or decolonization. Unsurprisingly, these platforms celebrate the same *types* of black activists and "thinkers" who confirm the world as they know it.

I would argue that black folks in particular have one of the most vulnerable identities in the United States because we don't know much about our past, and it makes us feel that we have a deficit. So we cling tightly to a manufactured type of blackness invented in white supremacist USA. I would even argue that "blackness" itself has been imposed on black people. We cling to myths about what our ancestors did, what precolonial African society was like; we celebrate a diet that was born out of oppression because, to be honest, that's all we know.

As much as we hate white supremacy, we're also scared of moving forward into unknown territory because at least in a white supremacy we know the rules. Frustration, pain, and racial fatigue are familiar feelings and, when you have nothing else, they fill those emotional gaps. We know the oppressive streets we walk on, and we develop a type of Stockholm syndrome for white supremacist patriarchy that prevents us from fighting it fully. So, we end up becoming safe activists, only talking to white people because we are positioned as the experts of victimization and oppression. No one will question us when we talk about racism or sexism to white people because that's *our* experience, which has morphed into an identity.

When your history, languages, and traditions have been erased, you become vulnerable and start clinging to anything with some semblance of an identity, which is partially why many African Americans have a difficult time *unlearning* manufactured blackness. Learning a new framework requires you to leave the safety of the only identity you've ever known.

However, each moment we turn away from learning more about oppression or being exposed to new ideas that could change the direction of our movements, we are no longer activists. In that setup, we are just clinging even tighter to the architecture of white supremacy.

We need to radically reevaluate everything we've ever known about our own bodies, the bodies of the dominant class, and the bodies of nonhuman animals. We need to do this as everything we've ever learned has been within the confines of white supremacist patriarchy, so we can't be ignorant of that fact that our "opinions" of certain groups and the values we adopt are influenced by this system. We have to be mindful that this process won't be easy, either: we are essentially excavating our racialized bodies to examine what has been forced upon us.

"Animal" is a category that we shove certain bodies into when we want to justify violence against them, which is why animal liberation should concern all who are minoritized, because at any moment you can become an "animal" and be considered disposable.

Being a radical anti-racist activist isn't about regurgitating the same accepted knowledges over and over as much as it's about having the courage to learn more about the different contours of white supremacy, which show up in spaces such as our food choices and attitudes toward other vulnerable groups. Being radical requires you to be uncomfortable, exposing yourself to new ideas that challenge the frameworks you operate through. Being radical is about asking the tough questions, engaging with different worldviews, and prizing critical thinking over popularity.

We will subvert white supremacist USA by not adopting its principles—in fact, it's radical *never* to believe what white supremacist USA tells you about yourself and other groups. If the dominant class is lying about black folks—telling everyone that we're lazy, that we have no culture, and so forth—imagine what they have invented about animals: that they can't feel pain, God put them here for us to eat, they have no culture, and so on.

This intertwined supremacism is precisely why I believe Afrofuturism, and not intersectionality, is the framework minoritized people need in order to generate real change. Intersectionality is a wonderful and useful tool to help oppressed folks navigate *current* systems of oppression that we never created, but it was never designed to map out the future. This is, in part, why some movements that claim to be "intersectional" feel stagnant; they keep dogmatically regurgitating the same analyses. Many intersectional movements assume liberation rests in finding newer intersections of oppression and creating new terms to add to the lexicon of oppression. These activists tend to replicate cosmetic diversity under the guise of intersectionality.

Unfortunately, intersectionality doesn't really trouble the systems looming over us that we never created. Intersectionality maps out the world that has been *imposed* on us; it doesn't begin the process of mapping out the future. Most importantly, intersectionality deals with the external conditions of racism and oppression that impact our lives, but doesn't speak to the internal struggles that arise after colonization.

As an activist who has been doing intersectional work for a long time, I remember how I started to feel trapped in the movements that were in front of me: I was interested in going forward. I felt that I recognized "isms" that were looming over me, but I didn't feel empowered to do anything about it. I felt that all I could do was talk about white people, teach white people, and point out white people's flaws. I wanted to move to a different model where I could use my creativity to find a way out. I wanted to liberate myself from internal fracturing.

I found a Tumblr post that articulated exactly how I felt:

> While I understood that defining and understanding the impacts of colonialism on the colonized was the first step to recovery and healing from the scars of such a system, I equally needed some resolve. I longed for the next step—a road map to becoming a decolonized being, beyond recognizing one's limitations. What did such a being look like? How did they sound? Did they even exist, in the West? Afrofuturism became the answer to all the questions above and more. . . . Exploring the richness of Afrofuturism, the study and cultural movement, I found my Mecca. I discovered what blackness could look like in the outer limits.[4]

Afrofuturism is important to our survival as people who are oppressed because it allows us to imagine beyond the confines of the dominant system. Most importantly, it allows us to float in new conceptual terrain, to have the courage to start the process of imagining newer ways of discussing phenomena, and newer ways of approaching oppression and liberation.

We have placed too much hope in the dominant class, and we need to realize that this is, in part, a product of being colonized. We're waiting around for the dominant class to "get it" rather than trusting our own imaginative sensibilities. Afrofuturism relies on the black creative imagination to make change and to carve out future worlds for ourselves on our own terms.

According to popular Afrofuturist Ytasha L. Womack, "Afrofuturism is often the umbrella for an amalgamation of narratives, but at the core, it values the power of creativity and imagination to reinvigorate culture and transcend social limitations. The resilience of the human spirit lies in our ability to imagine. The imagination is a tool of resistance."[5]

Afrofuturism is a departure from our past, which has been written by white supremacy. Although we might feel a deficit in terms of knowing who we are because of slavery and colonization, these actions have ironically forced us to rewrite ourselves and find newer ways of resisting the dominant power structures, which is something that the dominant class didn't expect. I no longer want or need white supremacy to tell me who I am, what I'm allowed to do, and who I'm allowed to be. I have the power to rewrite myself and my narrative.

Part of the power of the dominant society is in being able to take away your imagination such that the way the world is given to you is the only way it can ever be, and the only movement you can make within that setup is to get comfortable within it.

In order for black people (or any oppressed minority) to dismantle the system, we first need to dismantle it within ourselves, in the ways that we're trained to understand our bodies as well as other oppressed bodies.

Afrofuturism is about carving out a new type of blackness that isn't captive to white supremacist definitions. Right now in our anti-racist movements, as I explored in chapter 2, we spend time fighting the ways the dominant class depicts us. We exhaust all of our energy fighting what they say, how they react, which groups they give attention to, and so on. Afrofuturism is a departure from that setup.

In our anti-racist movements today, we often implicitly act as if white people are at the center of our social universe and we are just bodies that orbit them. This is erroneous and problematic in multiple ways, and an analogy may be useful in illustrating why this is the case.

Our contemporary society and even our social justice movements could be said to resemble the geocentric model of the universe, where the sun and the other celestial bodies orbit the earth. The geocentric model is, of course, false, but it was used for hundreds of years to explain and predict the movements of the celestial bodies seen in the sky, such as the planets and the sun. Yet it was also used to support a European religious ideology that sought to construe the universe as orbiting the earth. The geocentric model was used as a tool to assert a white-dominant world-view that was ordained by God(s). This was an extremely arrogant and human-centric articulation of the universe. After several hundred years, scientists (e.g., Copernicus) realized that the geocentric model was false and that the earth in fact revolves around the sun and is not the center of the solar system. So, in reality, and for the purposes of this analogy, the earth revolves around the sun and *needs* the sun in order for life to flourish and grow.

In some of our current mainstream social justice movements, many people may perhaps intuitively assume that white folks are at the center of the social solar system. Though, much like the geocentric model, this assumption may be observationally supportable in that everything appears to be orbiting whiteness (i.e., the earth), the reality is that white supremacy orbits a disempowered aggregate (i.e., the sun), and the disempowered are actually at the center of the system.

We need to change the way we view the social solar system and our relations within it, which in reality more accurately resembles the heliocentric model, whereby *we* don't orbit whiteness, but white supremacy orbits black people and all other beings labeled "inferior" in order to exist, grow, and thrive. There is no white supremacy if there is no antiblackness; there is no human if there is no animal. This cosmological analogy could perhaps be seen as illustrating Frantz Fanon's argument that "It is the racist who creates the inferiorized,"[6] and put another way by James Baldwin.[7]

We also need to realize that what connects us all as oppressed people is our assignment to the aggregated space of the subhuman or nonhuman. Drawing upon the heliocentric model, we are the sun. We form a coalition of all beings who deviate from the white/cis-/able-bodied heterosexual man, which we have been taught over and over again is the Human.

We need to realize just how powerful we are in the current system. We are the gravitational anchor and the central focus of the social solar system and to think or act otherwise only serves to maintain a tradition of racism, to say the least. Thus, the work is not necessarily in changing the dominant class or educating them, but reacquainting ourselves with our bodies so we fundamentally understand that we are not "less than" or inferior. We have nothing to prove. Our goal isn't merely to dethrone whiteness so that blackness takes its seat. We are striving for a social system that does not institute oppressive ideologies as the standard, and the social solar system analogy used here may be seen as a tool toward that end. When minoritized people understand that our collective inferiority is fictional, the energy we have been using to disprove our inferiority and show our humanity will no longer be necessary.

Once this is realized, we can reimagine citizenship for ourselves as well as for animals and other beings labeled "inferior." Moreover, as long as animals are oppressed, as long as "animal" means something degrading, we will never be set free. The inferiorized should be the authors of the change because we have an intimate understanding of what it means to be the subhuman aggregate.

Afrofuturism is our key to starting this process. Afrofuturism is about reimagining our citizenship as well as the citizenship of others, without being held captive by the thoughts of the dominant class. Our liberatory model comes from within us rather than around us in conditions that we didn't make. It's about realizing the vastness and expansiveness of our potential and possibilities.

This is why I think black veganism is an Afrofuturistic praxis.[8] People who have been oppressed and minoritized are actively challenging white supremacy by rearticulating their relationship to literal nonhuman animals. We are *also* developing a new relationship to "animal" as a social category that we have been placed in by white supremacy. We are radically prioritizing our own imaginations in a society that perpetually works to distract us so that we don't have time to think and create. Toni Morrison writes:

> [K]now the function, the very serious function of racism, which is distraction. It keeps you from doing your work. It keeps you explaining, over and over again, your reason for being. Somebody says you have no language, and so you spend twenty years proving that you do. Somebody says your head isn't shaped properly, so you have scientists working on the fact that it is. Somebody says you have no art, so you dredge that up. Somebody says that you have no kingdoms, and so you dredge that up. None of that is necessary. There will always be one more thing.[9]

Part of Afrofuturistic activism is realizing that the fight we're in today is supposed to be temporary. The problem with many intersectional activists today is they get so caught up in these systems and in fighting that they don't spend time grappling with *why* they're fighting. Many fight without having any clue as to what they want the world to look like one day. When we don't have a map for what we want our future to look like, we're fighting only because it makes us feel we have an identity.

As I always say, one day we have to climb out of our trenches and start building the world that we've always dreamed about, and we need to start working today on conceptual blueprints for that world. Afrofuturism gives us the space and time to start working on it.

Activism is merely a tool to help facilitate our right to imagine and our right to exist. However, my goal isn't to be an activist my whole life. I am merely trying to find new conceptual territory to build a new world where I can breathe and relax. At the end of the day, having the ability to exist, to breathe, to create, to relax, and to love is something we should all be able to do effortlessly. As long as that's not a reality for certain living beings, I will continue fighting.

I'm going to close with a quote from Ytasha Womack:

Hope, much like imagination, comes at a premium. The cost is a life where more is expected. Where more is expected, new actions are required. The audacity of hope, the bold declaration to believe, and clarity of vision for a better life and world are the seeds to personal growth, revolutionized societies, and life-changing technologies.[10]

AFTERWORD

I AM HONORED AND HUMBLED BY THE OPPORTUNITY TO BE A SMALL PART of this important book from these two amazing sisters. Writing the afterword does not mean I get the last word; it means I get to listen and reflect before I offer a few words after Aph and Syl's words. I use the word *listen* because of Aph and Syl's style of communicating with each other, a conversation they have invited us to join. They have modeled for us how to respond to these ideas: it takes time; we need to respect the other's turn at speaking; we need not be defensive.

Each of us as readers has the opportunity to join the conversation. First, we listen to the rhythm and force of their words as they share their insights. Then come "after" words.

Before I answer who this *we* is of which I speak, let me answer who this *I* is who speaks. I'm an anti-racist white vegan feminist and author of *The Sexual Politics of Meat*. In that book, published in 1989, I talk about the concept of "interconnected oppressions," and address what I see as "the racial politics of meat" as part of patriarchal dominance. During the 1980s, when I working on my book, I was involved as chair of the housing committee of the local NAACP in a nearly ten-year fight for integrated housing in a small upstate New York town. In the campaign, I had to confront my naïveté about racism. I thought that if we proponents explained that one's property values don't decline when public housing is built—and public housing in this city was equated with "blacks moving into the neighborhood"—the whites who were against the housing would listen and would stop protesting. I was shocked by the comments made at public meetings and on a local radio program as whites engaged in racist hate speech. I began to augment even more my reading of African American history, fiction, and literary and political theory to try to understand the reasons for the raw racist politics of that city.

The activist self of the 1980s could not have anticipated the developments of these past few years: the numbers of African Americans killed by the police, the overt racism of an entire political party, a man who becomes US Attorney General *despite* a racist record. But the two women you've just read would have anticipated these developments. At this time we need the clarity of thought and incisive words of writers like the incredible sister duo, Aph and Syl Ko.

1. The Importance of Critical Theory

To begin with, Aph and Syl demonstrate the importance of critical theory. Critical theory is engaged theory; it understands bodies are at risk; it is informed by activism and it is written, in part, to inform activism. Critical theory is not detached; it does not presume an objective knowledge stance because it understands there is no such position.

Aph and Syl offer a "new conceptual architecture" that is invitational, that situates itself, that understands and is indebted to what preceded it, but looks forward. It's deconstructive and reconstructive and liberating, as the writers resituate the focus from who the oppressed are to the commonalities of the oppressor. How do they do this?

First, they introduce black veganism as "a sociopolitical movement that rearticulates black oppression through the lens of animality and race" (Aph). "Black veganism is a *methodological tool* to reactivate our imaginations" (Syl). This tool can bring down the master's house. "Racism is simultaneously anti-*black* and anti-*animal*, as seen by racial ideology's elevation and celebration of 'the human' and 'humanity' particularly as Western and *white*" (Syl).

They are building, as Syl says, "on a very long tradition of black and brown thinkers, activists, scholars, citizen-intellectuals, and artists who have, from the beginning, seen the human–animal binary in effect in racial oppression." But she wishes to examine the animal aspect of the binary. Just as Aimé Césaire in *Discourse on Colonialism* claimed that the Negro had been "an invention of Europe," so, "the category *animal* was also a colonial invention that has been imposed on humans and animals." Syl continues, "So, the 'human' or what 'humanity' is just is *a conceptual way to mark the province of European whiteness as the ideal way of being homo sapiens.* This means that the conceptions of 'humanity/human' and 'animality/animal' have been constructed along *racial* lines." As a result, "animals did not inform our notion of 'animality.' 'Animality' informed our notions of animals."

Aph elaborates: "Assuming animals are disposable is actually a product of being colonized by white supremacist patriarchy." Eurocentric veganism distorts our ability to hear Aph and Syl by creating a vegan practice that uses comparisons, analogies, and discussions of similarities in treatment that elide differences in oppressive practices and structures. Racist oppression is not an *example* to be exploited for the liberation of the other animals. The Eurocentric vegan practice of lifting up the experience of people who have been animalized as a *metaphor* for another's (the animals') oppression makes the experiences of oppressed people disappear as materially relevant. In the language of my critical theory, this contributes to the absent referent status of black victims of white supremacy.

In *The Sexual Politics of Meat*, I argued that the structure of the absent referent functions to cause the disappearance of the animals who become flesh and whose bodies produce dairy and eggs. But I suggested as well that non-dominant people also become absent referents in a white patriarchal world. Comparisons and analogies generalize away particularities; they do not liberate, because an aspect of the absent referent remains absent, sacrificed as metaphor to illustrate another being's oppression. Aph says, "[T]he racial grammar of the [vegan] movement is white." Using the effects of white supremacy on black people as a comparison with what the other animals suffer is one example of this grammar.

Eurocentric veganism cannot correct systemic racism, but the problem is that some Eurocentric vegans never perceived dismantling racism as part of their mandate. One of Aph's goals, she writes, was "to de-center white-centric campaigns that normally came to people's mind when *anyone* talked about blackness and animality. In other words, I was getting tired of paying the cost for some white people fucking up the conversation."

I have been reading Mary Helen Washington's *The Other Blacklist: The African American Literary and Cultural Left of the 1950s* while reading Aph and Syl. Washington, the editor of remarkable anthologies of black women's writings, including *Black-Eyed Susans: Classic Stories by and about Black Women*, describes growing up in the 1950s, and her Catholic black girl's education. She writes:

> The worst epithet we could use to describe racial discrimination was the anemic term "prejudice"; we didn't know then that race militants and leftists called it, more accurately, "white supremacy," they make clear that there was an organized racialized structure based on political, economic, and social oppression, not just bad white behavior, and that the goal for black equality was not only changing minds and hearts but challenging institutions.[1]

Framing white supremacy as "prejudice" explains why some whites become defensive when asked to become aware of their white privilege. Thinking the conversation is about "prejudice," they take it personally, missing the systemic analysis. Catalyzed by Washington's distinctions and Aph and Syl's analysis, I created this chart to help us identify the radical resituating of the discussion that has occurred in this book:

(1) Critical Theory	(2) Depoliticized Privilege of Some Form
It's white supremacy	It's "prejudice"—results in defensiveness
Systemic	Personal—unable to think themselves out of the individualized explanation, results in guilt

Critical thinking/ epistemological revolution	Framework that can't be disturbed (for instance, animal oppression should be understood in terms of "speciesism")
Decenters whiteness in vegan theory	Why introduce race as an issue? "Helping the animals"
Whiteness informs definition of human–animal	Whiteness unlinked to animal oppression
Decolonize antiracist and animal advocacy thinking	It's about "diversity," reproducing the conditions that created the original problems
Human–animal binary aspect to racist logic	Analogies that inadequately reflect reality, exploit one oppression in seeking another's liberation
Theory that links animality and white supremacy and misogyny	Separate issues: "helping the animals" or feminism or black liberation. Don't confuse issues
Multiple ways of veganism	The right way (and the right body) to be vegan
Disruptive	Comforting

2. What Does Critical Theory Ask of Us?

Aph and Syl's critical theory asks us to listen. In the midst of the cacophony of our time, when we are all instant experts with opinions, comments, and tweets: *listen*. To begin with, they were listening to each other. They model listening with respect to each other, and in their writing an ongoing invitational style is sustained.

Don't just listen: *ponder.* Syl comments:

Sometimes it doesn't occur to us that the unglamorous work of thinking about and discussing *how* we should do something about some problem *is* doing something about the problem. It's only by discussing and thinking about how that problem arises, how it presents itself, how it's maintained, that we start to locate what the problem *is.* And oftentimes, the problem looks starkly different from when those discussions first began.

Aph and Syl took their time with the thoughts expressed in this book. They were doing something: they talked, discussed, explored, wrote, revisited, revised.

Don't just ponder: *reflect.* Bring these ideas into your hearts and minds, and live with their insights. We have so much to learn (and unlearn), but we are animals who learn (and can unlearn).

Learning with openness involves hearing their new framework for talking about animality and race, not simplifying, not making comparisons, not responding defensively. If you find yourself doing that— simplifying, comparing, and refusing to hear or challenging their right to speak, and feeling defensive and guilty—you have privatized a political and theoretical conversation.

3. Multiple Audiences for *Aphro-ism*

Rereading the manuscript over the past few weeks, I recognized the multiple audiences for this book.

For all who identify with Black Vegans Rock: here is a keystone theory, like the stone that holds up an arch. Black Vegans Rock is a way of thinking that lifts us up *so* we can see, and holds us in place *as* we see.

For those who resist bringing animals into an analysis of white male supremacy because it is thought that this will distract from progressive, antiracist, feminist work: here is a critical theory that argues the opposite. We cannot do our progressive, antiracist, feminist work without an understanding of the interaction of race, gender, and animality. This understanding doesn't dilute our work; it empowers it. *"Our mainstream social justice movements are doomed so long as Eurocentric theory is used to structure the logic of these movements"* (Aph). In other words, the human–animal binary implicit in the philosophy that shapes and upholds modernity provides us with a very special and particular justification to use and abuse animals as we see fit.

Although many different societies prior to and alongside modern Westernized and colonized cultures use (and used) animals, the Western colonial justification is its own unique kind. For progressives who distance themselves from or refuse to consider the analysis of how race, gender, and animality interact to structure the permissibility of eating animals and dairy and eggs, and using animals, animals remain absent referents. As Syl says, the *"open acceptance of the negative status of 'the animal' . . . is a tacit acceptance of the hierarchical racial system and white supremacy in general."*

For animal ethics (philosophy): Instead of dwelling on *literal* animals and their capacities, Aph and Syl shift the ethical debate to the realm of social ontology. They ask us to reflect on what it means to argue for or against obligations and rights when it comes to beings who are already "doomed" to a certain status by social codification. Aph and Syl draw together the biological human–animal binary (which disadvantages nonhuman animals) and the social human–animal binary (which disadvantages many humans) and argue that the latter subsumes the former.

For critical animal studies: Aph and Syl open up so many possibilities, I am only going to identify a few, but I'm excited for this field because of what this book can mean for future efforts.

- **Literary criticism:** In 1988, the path-breaking *The Signifying Monkey: A Theory of Afro-American Literary Criticism* by Henry Louis Gates Jr. was published to wide acclaim. Gates is concerned, in part, with the "search of the black subject for a textual voice," and examines monkey tales (the monkey is a trickster figure in West African literary traditions) as they represent speech acts.[2] If Aph and Syl's understanding of the connections between race and animality were brought to this study, what new insights might arise from this already powerful book in terms of monkeys having a voice?

- **Environmental history**: Robust works on environmental history are enriching our understanding. I think, for instance, of *The Republic of Nature: An Environmental History of the United States* by Mark Fiege or *Creatures of Empire: How Domestic Animals Transformed Early America* by Virginia DeJohn Anderson. How would adding "animality" as an aspect of colonialism and enslavement of peoples deepen these already supple and important analyses?

- **Political theory**: Aph and Syl challenge political theorists to create a theory that does not sacrifice the animal, animality, and animals in arguing for disenfranchised people.

- **Natural history**: We need non-speciesist, non-racist, non-sexist discussions of evolution. For instance, *The Book That Changed America: How Darwin's Theory of Evolution Ignited a Nation* by Randall Fuller has been criticized for omitting discussion of how African American thinkers responded to Darwin's theories. Eric Foner points out that writers for the black press "cited 'On the Origin of Species' as proof of mankind's 'progressive development,' which would lead inevitably to the abolition of slavery."[3] How were understandings both of animality and race changed by Darwin?

- **Abolitionist and antislavery history**:—especially the new focus on interrelated activisms found, for instance, in Manisha Sinha's *The Slave's Cause: A History of Abolition*. How would these histories be changed by including animals as well as the other transnational activisms Sinha identifies aligned with abolitionism: feminism, utopian socialism, anti-imperialism, and labor activism?

- **Feminist scholarship** could focus on gender, race, and animality in literature, history, and philosophy while resisting Eurocentric ways of presenting these ideas.

For vegans of all colors: Many will welcome this book because it provides the conceptual architecture for something they have intuited. But some may resist the idea that veganism has anything to do with political issues, especially race and gender.

In specific, some white vegans are doing to black vegan theorists and activists what nonvegans do to vegans. They are so sure of their own opinions: saying *this* isn't an issue; challenging "Why are you raising this concern?"; waiting for the moment to interrupt; becoming defensive, minimizing, dismissing, challenging, and accusing, until they become "trolls." Instead, listen to Aph and Ko the way you would like a nonvegan to listen to you, with respect for you because you have thought about the problem, have researched what you know, and trust your solution. Also, stop making comparisons, stop protesting that it's not #blacklivesmatter but #alllivesmatter, making those who are victims of white supremacy absent referents.

If nonvegans respond to vegans protesting, "What about the homeless? What about battered women? What about racism?" and so on, using a narrow social-justice focus that misses this analysis, some vegans mimic the response by saying of their activism the opposite ("It's *only* about the animals"), erasing systemic oppression from their consideration. Thus, they focus on animals without placing their status within the context of the modern West's fetishization, glorification, and empowerment of white men. How do we help the other animals if we fail to understand the source of their oppression?

Here is a book that can help the vegan movement become what it's potentially able to be.

In 1993, in an essay entitled "Beastliness and the Politics of Solidarity" in *Neither Man Nor Beast*, I speculated that some white animal activists were willing to deal with their human privilege over the other animals as they conceived of it but not their racial or sexual privilege because their notion of "human" excluded an understanding of how race and gender informed its definition. Some vegans want a de-racialized veganism that is a lie, clinging to the idea that animals "need" us most and so making white privilege disappear. All of dominant culture has allowed for this reductionist reaction. Suggestion: look at the chart on p. 142. Where are your views represented? If you find them on the right side, reread this book. Let us, as Aph suggests, "form a coalition of all beings who deviate from the white/cis-/able-bodied heterosexual man—which we have been taught over and over again is the Human."

4. The Challenge of Our Time

The period we are living in offers us an opportunity to create responses that get to the heart of domination. I think of the opportunities of the past like Reconstruction—"America's first experiment with interracial democracy after the Civil War."[4] But the United States turned from being committed to justice for the formerly enslaved to a mythos of "reunion" in which "the Old and New south were romanticized and welcomed back to a new nationalism, and in which devotion alone made everyone right, and no one truly wrong." As the "endearing mutuality of sacrifice among soldiers" came to dominate national memory, "another process was at work—the denigration of black dignity and the attempted erasure of emancipation from the national narrative of what the war had been about."

In the midst of the Civil Rights movement, the observation of the centennial of the Civil War offered an opportunity to tell the history correctly and bring it up to date: that the war was about slavery, that Jim Crow laws were abominations, and that what the country needed was a new Emancipation Proclamation. Instead, a deracinated, flattened story of "brothers all" (that ignored the fighting of black troops) prevailed. As a result, "the process by which the nation and the states remembered the struggle of the 1860s enhanced and exploited the racial divisions of the 1960s more than it helped to alleviate them."[5]

The refusal to name accurately is dangerous. It has resulted twice in the United States in a choice of white unity that covers over racial oppression and white supremacy. At those epochal moments in the United States, justice for all lost to a false and inadequate notion of unity.

We are in such an epochal moment now. Will we move toward justice or replicate the same white supremacy issues that favor "unity" with a progressive face? Will veganism be understood through this lens of race and animality as the radical social justice movement it is? Will progressives, anti-racists, feminists, LGBTQIA and black liberationists—all those who constitute the mighty resistance of this time—recognize how human privilege is woven into white male supremacy? It's a critical moment. Now is the time for us to listen to and embrace black veganism.

Carol J. Adams
April 2017

Acknowledgments

Aph

First and foremost, I would like to say thank you to my husband, Wes. It is rare to have a partner who is brilliant, insightful, patient, smart, and supportive. He is my *very* best friend, and he has spent hours upon hours listening to me rant (filibuster-style) about social problems; he has spent night after night watching me practice my speeches, while providing valuable feedback; and he has never, ever given up on me. He has even extended some of my own ideas. He has been by my side through the biggest highs and lows of my life, and I love him dearly. Without him, this book wouldn't be a reality. He continues to show me what unconditional love looks like. He reminds me throughout all of this activist work that the most important thing in life is family.

Thank you to my brilliant sister Syl. Without her guidance, intelligence, love, and brilliance, *Aphro-ism* wouldn't exist. Thank you for having the courage to extend my mind and converse with me about these subjects for over a decade. I have always felt lucky to have you as a sister.

Thank you to Martin Rowe and everyone at Lantern for believing in this book and publishing our words.

I would also like to thank some of my *dearest* digital friends, including Dr. Amie Breeze Harper, who has been helping me cultivate my voice for years; lauren Ornelas, whose humor and support has given me courage to continue on in this movement; and Christopher Sebastian McJetters, who has been wonderfully supportive of my projects. Thanks to Justin Van Kleeck, Pax Ahimsa Gethen, and Charlotte Eure for always being there when I need someone to talk to. Special thanks to Valerie McGowan for being supportive of my work and helping me manage Black Vegans

Rock. I would like to say a *huge* thank you to Tracye McQuirter, MPH, for providing me with incredible opportunities and guidance; Dr. Milton Mills for his remarkable medical knowledge; Stephanie Redcross for giving me business advice; Demetrius Bagley for always encouraging my work; as well as Dr. Corey Lee Wrenn for cultivating my voice years ago on Vegan Feminist Network. I will never forget the hilarious conversations we had throughout the years. Your support made my grad school experience much more enjoyable.

I would like to say thank you to Dr. Aisha Durham, my *incredible* graduate adviser, who helped me become the activist I am today. She always appreciated my quirky, nerdy, awkward ways. You knew how to work around my anxieties to pull the best work out of me. Some other grad school professors who changed my life are Dr. Rachel Dubrofsky, Dr. Ambar Basu, Dr. Mahuya Pal, and Dr. Abe Khan. Amazing undergrad professors include Mamie Hixon (who gave me the most wonderful opportunity to participate in the Harlem Renaissance play), Roz Fisher, Dr. Katherine Romack, and Dr. Brendan and Tressa Kelly (who suggested I go to graduate school for communication).

I would also like to thank Dawn Moncrief of A Well-Fed World, who has supported my work and had the courage to amplify my voice when others were trying to silence it. I would also like to give a shout out to new friends for their encouragement: Seba Johnson, Richard Bowie, pattrice jones, David and Paige Carter, Unique Vance, Aaron Luxur, Brenda Sanders, Jasmine Leyva, Naijha Wright-Brown, Nzinga Young, Jenné Claiborne, Keith Tucker, Carol J. Adams, and Dr. Lori Gruen. I would also like to thank Jacqueline Olive, who provided me with an unbelievable opportunity to work on a powerful film. *Always in Season* helped me to understand the role of reconciliation in the process of healing.

I would like to say a *big* thank you to Alise and Jack of Eastrand Studios who created the book cover. They also made the art for Black Vegans Rock, and I appreciate their hard work and unique ability to make me feel confident, even when I don't know what the hell I'm doing. I cherish our conversations that are always filled with laughter, exciting details, and random funny stories. Their talent is *beyond* real, and they always find a way of capturing and extending my imagination.

I need to send shout outs to personal friends who have stood by my side for years: Eszter Zimányi . . . what can I even say? Since high school you've kept up with me and supported me. I cherish our friendship and your super smart brain. Lisa Spinazola . . . GURL . . . can we be related already? Thank you for such an incredible time during graduate school from BGC sleepovers to dance parties in our office. Special shout out to Kyle Romano (whose dry humor served as my fuel for survival during grad school), as well as Ariane Anderson, who is one of the quirkiest and most inimitable individuals I have ever met. Thank you to Monica and Brenda Coleman, who made my undergrad years memorable. I will always treasure the dinners we shared as well as the probing conversations that changed my life.

Last, but definitely not least, I would like to say a special thank you to my huge family: Jane, Syl, Dules, and Ram—you all rock. I'm lucky to have supportive siblings like you who serve as excellent role models. Dez— you are the coolest niece and I hope that when you get older, you read this book and get brainwashed! I would like to send a shout out to Karen, Barry, Abby, and Ally, who have been by my side for almost a decade. I appreciate the vegan dinners and how willing you are to embrace me as a member of your family. Huge shout out to Kathy, AG, Peggy, and Lee who made my undergraduate years absolutely astounding. I spent some of my best holidays with you all and you helped shape me into the person that I am. To Grandma Jessie, I love you and I'm glad that we've reconnected after all of these years. I'm happy to know that you are eighty-one years strong!! Thank you, Aunt Mary, for being supportive and always taking time to be a part of my life.

Here's a special thank you to my mother, who defied all odds to raise five brilliant children and still live happily and fully—#outie2017. You have taught me that life is what you make it . . . literally. You showed me what real happiness looks like, and you always remind me that being an independent woman who has her shit together is the definition of empowerment! Your unconditional love inspires me each day and I'm lucky that I have someone to call up whenever I need a good laugh or a shoulder to cry on. Thank you, Carl, for being a wonderful stepfather. I love your advice and motivational speeches and, most importantly, I will always remember, "Do you."

I would finally like to say rest in peace to my father, who passed away while I was working on this book. I feel your presence watching over me each day. I feel inspired by your creativity and courage to follow your dreams and provide for a family along the way. I hope you are proud of what Syl and I have accomplished together. I love you and miss you, and know that I will always be proud of you. You have encouraged me more than you will ever know to pursue my own truth and to never, ever be afraid to share my voice. I love you.

Syl

I'd like to thank Aph for inviting me to contribute to *Aphro-ism*. Thanks for so many years of friendship, challenging discussions, and love. Thank you to my family for their encouragement and support as we worked on this project: Dorothy and Carl, Virginia and Hunter, Wesley, Juliet and Anders, and Ramses. I'd also like to acknowledge those of you who supported my work by talking through it with me, presenting objections or suggesting ideas, recommending literature and artwork, and/or integrating my views into your own. There are so many of you, but I'd like to specifically thank Ryan Preston-Roedder, Douglas Maclean, Rebecca Walker, Steve Wise, Kevin Schneider, Jason Wyckoff, Frédéric Côté-Boudreau, Francesco Yugiro Asano, Joi Cox, and the philosophy graduate students at UNC–Chapel Hill. A special thanks to Krasimira Filcheva, Linda and Alan Nelson, Katherine Kershaw, James DeAlto, Amani Michael, Christine Wells, Lori Gruen, Helen Sakkaris, Allison Sherman, Molly Josephson, and Lok Chan. I could not have completed the final essays without the help of Philip Maier. I extend to you immense gratitude. I am deeply appreciative of Martin Rowe for his time and patience in sending us feedback, suggestions, and edits. And last, but not least, thank you to my father, Józef, who brought me to love animals and philosophy passionately.

NOTES

Authors' Note

I. The term *decolonial* has different definitions; however, I regard it as an *epistemic de-linking*, or *epistemic disobedience*, as described by Aníbal Quijano and Walter Mignolo. Mignolo writes: "Decoloniality is therefore the energy that does not allow the operation of the logic of coloniality nor believes the fairy tales of the rhetoric of modernity.... [D]ecolonial thinking is, then, thinking that de-links and opens ... to the possibilities hidden ... by the modern rationality that is mounted and enclosed by categories of Greek, Latin, and the six modern imperial European languages." See Walter D. Mignolo. "Epistemic Disobedience and the Decolonial Option: A Manifesto," *Transmodernity: Journal of Peripheral Cultural Production of the Luso-Hispanic World*, Vol I. No. 2 (Fall 2011): 44–66.

1. Black Lives, Black Life

1. George Jackson. *Soledad Brother: The Prison Letters of George Jackson* (Chicago: Lawrence Hill Books, 1994), 289.

2. Jenevieve Ting. "Angela Davis's Legacy of Collective Solidarity," *Ms.* magazine blog. Last modified February 26, 2015 <http://msmagazine. com/blog/2015/02/26/angela-daviss-legacy-of-collective-solidarity/>.

3. Aimé Césaire. *Discourse on Colonialism*, tr. Joan Pinkham (New York: Monthly Review Press, 2000).

2. Bringing Our Digital Mops Home

1. White feminism is a type of feminism that excludes intersectional analyses. For more information, visit, Julie Zeilinger: "The Brutal Truth Every White Feminist Needs to Hear," *Mic*, September 11, 2015 <https://mic. com/articles/125084/the-brutal-truth-every-white-feminist-needs-to-hear#.NxSsoIwYV>.

2. I was first introduced to the term *minoritized* in graduate school. My adviser, Dr. Aisha Durham, used this word instead of *minority* because, she stated, institutions are *actively* engaging with the process of minoritizing people. *Minority* (as a label) puts the burden on the people marked as "different" rather than shifting the focus to the institutions that are engaging in this process of ensuring that certain populations remain disenfranchised.

3. It's important to note just how problematic it is that people of color and people of nonconforming gender identities are merely regarded as "toppings" on the cheese pizza in Hughes' analogy. This analogy suggests that the standard, naturalized, and dominant template of womanhood is a cis-heterosexual-white woman (seen as the cheese pizza), and the rest of us are seen as having "extra," supplementary identities (through the deluxe pizza narrative). The analogy goes against the basic tenets of intersectionality itself, which positions minoritized women as having their own unique experience, whereas Hughes' video casts minoritized women as white women with more diversity.

4. Britni Danielle. "Maybe Black People Should Dress Like Lions, or How Cecil the Lion Has Gotten More Sympathy than Dead Black People," *Clutch.* Retrieved from <http://www.clutchmagonline.com/2015/07/maybe-black-people-should-dress-like-lions-or-how-cecil-the-lion-has-gotten-more-sympathy-than-dead-black-people/>.

5. Roxane Gay. "Of Lions and Men: Mourning Samuel DuBose and Cecil the Lion," *New York Times*, August 1, 2015 <http://www.nytimes.com/2015/08/01/opinion/of-lions-and-men-mourning-samuel-dubose-and-cecil-the-lion.html?_r=0>.

6. *Dear White People* is a satirical film written and directed by Justin Simien. The film centers on several black protagonists who are experiencing racial tensions at an Ivy League campus. Some critics of the film stated that the humor was too obvious and recentered the white gaze. Although the film attempts to cater to black audiences, it inevitably ended up pandering to white viewers.

7. Racial Discussion Fatigue Syndrome (RDFS) is based on a video that Akilah Hughes created in reference to the exhaustion of people of color after engaging in debates with racist white people online. It appears as though RDFS is based on Racial Battle Fatigue Syndrome, which was coined by

Dr. William A. Smith, who was interested in looking at the ways that racial microaggressions in institutions (particularly academia) adversely affect the health and achievements of students of color.

8. Zeba Blay. "Why We Need to Talk about White Feminism," *Huffington Post*, August 10, 2015 <http://www.huffingtonpost.com/entry/why-we-need-to-talk-about-white-feminism_us_55c8ca5ce4b0f73b20ba020a>.

9. Roxane Gay. Twitter post, July 29, 2015, 8:44 A.M. <https://twitter.com/rgay/status/626418037810425856>.

10. I added this point after a conversation with Syl about the ways that disciplinary thinking (being forced to filter your experiences through one lens) can create borders around your own oppression and prevent you from adequately being able to articulate what your oppression is.

3. #AllVegansRock

1. Aph Ko. "#BlackVegansRock: 100 Black Vegans to Check Out," *Striving with Systems*, June 11, 2015 <https://strivingwithsystems.com/2015/06/11/blackvegansrock-100-black-vegans-to-check-out/>.

2. The conference predominantly featured vegan activists of color who shared their perspectives. I was awarded (with two other people) the Anti-racist Changemaker of the Year Award at this conference.

3. Aph Ko. "Black Folks Creating Spaces of Empowerment Isn't 'Segregation,'" *Wear Your Voice: Intersectional Feminist Media*, July 2, 2015 <http://wearyourvoicemag.com/identities/race/black-folks-creating-spaces-of-empowerment-isnt-segregation>.

4. The Vegan Society was also surprised at how many negative comments showed up. A representative from the society reached out to let me know the society supported me and apologized for the public reaction to the article. In fact, the society said my list produced some of the most "vile, hateful" comments ever seen on their Facebook page.

5. Anita Sarkeesian is a popular media critic and the founder of *Feminist Frequency*. She is known for creating short videos where she analyzes women's portrayals in popular culture. In 2012, she decided to do a series on sexism in video games and was faced with an onslaught of digital attacks from groups of men (now known as Gamergate) who threatened to rape and kill her just because she critiqued video games for their narrow, sexist portrayals of women.

4. By "Human," Everybody Just Means "White"

I. Esther Yu-Hsi Lee. "San Francisco Cops Said It Was Legal to Murder Black Man Because He Was an 'Animal,'" *Think Progress*, March 15, 2015 <http://thinkprogress. org/justice/2015/03/15/3633907/sfpd-deplorable-racist-emails/>.

2. Sylvia Wynter. "No Humans Involved: An Open Letter to My Colleagues," Forum N.H.I. Knowledge for the 21st Century, Vol. I, No.I (Fall 1994): 42–71. Retrieved from <http://carmenkynard.org/wp-content/ uploads/2013/07/No-Humans-Involved-An-Open-Letter-to-My-Colleagues-by-SYLVIA-WYNTER.pdf>.

3. Douglas MacLean. "Is 'Human Being' a Moral Concept?" *Philosophy & Public Policy Quarterly*, Vol. 30, Nos. 3/4 (Summer/Fall 2010) <http://journals. gmu.edu/PPPQ/article/viewFile/90/72>.

4. Walter D. Mignolo. "Who Speaks for the 'Human' in Human Rights?" *Human Rights in Latin American and Iberian Cultures*, Hispanic Issues Online 5.I (2009): 7–24 <https://cla.umn.edu/sites/cla.umn.edu/files/hiol_05_0I_ mignolo_who_speaks_for_the_22human22_in_22human_rights22.pdf>.

5. María Lugones. "Heterosexualism and the Colonial/Modern Gender System," Hypatia 22, No. I (2007): 186–209 <https://muse.jhu.edu/ article/206329>.

6. Oyèrónké Oyěwùmí. *The Invention of Women: Making an African Sense of Western Gender Discourses* (Minneapolis: University of Minnesota Press, 1997): 196.

7. Lugones, *op. cit.*: 190.

5. Why Confusion Is Necessary for Our Activism to Evolve

I. Tommy Curry. "The Eschatological Dilemma: The Problem of Studying the Black Male Only as the Deaths that Result from Anti-black Racism," in *I Am Because We Are: Readings in Africana Philosophy* edited by Fred Lee Hord and Jonathan Scott Lee (Amherst: University of Massachusetts Press, 2015): 479–500 <http://www.academia.edu/652263I/The_ Eschatological_Dilemma_The_Problem_of_Studying_the_Black_ Male_only_as_the_Deaths_that_Result_from_Anti-Black_Racism>.

2. Kristen Gwynne. "How 'Stop and Frisk' Is Too Often a Sexual Assault by Cops on Teenagers in Targeted NYC Neighborhoods," *Alternet*, January 2I, 2013 <http://www.alternet.org/civil-liberties/ how-stop-and-frisk-too-often-sexual-assault-cops-teenagers-targeted-nyc>.

3. J. M. Allain. "Sexual Relations between Elite White Women and Enslaved Men in the Antebellum South: A Socio-historical Analysis," *Inquiries*, Vol. 5, No. 8, 2013 <http://www.inquiriesjournal.com/articles/747/2/sexual-relations-between-elite-white-women-and-enslaved-men-in-the-antebellum-south-a-socio-historical-analysis>.

7. Emphasizing Similarities Does Nothing for the Oppressed

1. Robert Sussman. "There Is No Such Thing as Race," *Newsweek*, November 18, 2014 <http://www.newsweek.com/there-no-such-thing-race-283123>.

2. I am using "race," "racial differences," and so on in the most diluted way possible, obviously.

3. James McWilliams. "Beastly Justice," *Slate*, February 21, 2013 <http://www.slate.com/articles/life/history/2013/02/medieval_animal_trials_why_they_re_not_quite_as_crazy_as_they_sound.html>.

4. Ashley Capps. "Responding to the Claim that Animals Can't Reason, Don't Deserve Same Consideration," *Free from Harm*, December 29, 2014 <http://freefromharm.org/common-justifications-for-eating-animals/animals-cant-reason-dont-deserve-treatment/>.

5. From the introduction to Wolfe's *Animal Rites: American Culture, the Discourse of Species, and Posthumanist Theory* (University of Chicago Press, 2003). For those interested in the animal issue, Wolfe is a great resource. His philosophical work seeks to undermine the constant threat of humanism that appears even in animal rights discourse. For example, the first chapter of *Animal Rites* argues that "[o]ne of the central ironies of animal rights philosophy is that its philosophical framework remains essentially humanist in its most important philosophers (utilitarianism in Peter Singer, neo-Kantianism in Tom Regan), thus effacing the very difference of the animal other that it sought to respect" ("Old Orders for New: Ecology, Animal Rights, and the Poverty of Humanism," p. 8).

6. Marc Bekoff. "Animal Minds and the Foible of Human Exceptionalism," *Psychology Today*, July 30, 2011 <https://www.psychologytoday.com/blog/animal-emotions/201107/animal-minds-and-the-foible-human-exceptionalism?collection=67119>.

7. Of course, this is observable with lots of other phenomena as well, such as sexism.

8. Among *many* motivations, this is the one I'm interested in here.

9. I included the IQ consideration because it's such a hot-button issue for many people. Personally, though, I think IQ stuff is mostly nonsense.

10. Contrast this with the surrealist Aimé Césaire.

11. Cora Diamond. "Eating Meat and Eating People," *Philosophy*, Vol. 53, No. 206 (1978): 465–79 <https://ethicslab.georgetown.edu/phil145/wordpress/wp-content/uploads/2015/05/Diamond-Eating-Meat-and-Eating-People.pdf>.

12. That's not to say that the natural and the social sciences don't have their own problems when it comes to "studying" or "researching" beings; however, I won't go into this issue here.

13. I borrow this suggestion and phrasing from Walter Mignolo.

14. Wynter argues that the notion of "the objective human," which she describes as "the overrepresentation of man," must be uprooted if we are to ever unsettle coloniality (the long-lasting effects of white colonial rule). (She also believes this "biocentric" rendering of "the human" prevents us from settling the question of human consciousness, which is her primary concern.) As a result, she describes being human as *praxis* as opposed to a noun. See her article "Unsettling the Coloniality of Being/Power/Truth/Freedom: Towards the Human, After Man, Its Overrepresentation—An Argument," *CR: The New Centennial Review*, Vol. 3, No. 3 (Fall 2003): 257–337.

8. Addressing Racism Requires Addressing the Situation of Animals

1. In animal rights and vegan spaces, it is customary for members to draw on racism or racist practices, usually the transatlantic slave trade, as a way to draw a productive analogy between the situation of nonhuman animals and that of oppressed human groups. But these analogies are usually just that: analogies. Although some activists will make the profound point that these horrors are manifestations of the same system, they generally fail to make the point I am trying to make here: that racism and speciesism should not be treated independently of each other since speciesism *is* racial thinking.

2. See law professor Maneesha Deckha's *fantastic* paper: "The Subhuman as a Cultural Agent of Violence," *Journal for Critical Animal Studies*, Vol., No. 3 (2010): 28–51.

3. What I am suggesting is that [white human male] comprises a *single* category. So, I am *not* saying there are three categories that comprise the top level: [white] + [human] + [male]. Also, I think it's worth noting that, due to the Western obsession with individuality, plants and "nature" are generally missing from the scheme (or the [animal] is collapsed into the even more generic and insulting reduction of the complexity of different life forms: [nature]). Needless to say, the less "individuality" we perceive, the less is their moral worth. This sheds some light on why members of racialized groups protest that they are not seen as "individual," but rather as representative of their whole group. As I mention later, though, I'm not sure this protest works in our favor.

4. Deckha, *op. cit.*: 38.

5. Excerpt from Deckha: "[Sherene] Razack highlights the phenomenon of the 'camp'—spaces where states pass laws or take other measures to create a lawless zone untouched by rule of law principles." This is a "notable feature of many camps" today: "racialized individuals identified as terrorist or migrant threats and thus in need of containment and discipline" (34). Deckha goes on to note that Razack calls these spaces "state[s] of exception," and says that "the effect of the war on terror has been to discursively normalize these spaces and the violence they inflict" (35). Here is another relevant excerpt from Razack, quoted by Deckha (37):

> Although race thinking varies, for Muslims and Arabs, it is underpinned by the idea that modern enlightened, secular peoples must protect themselves from pre-modern, religious peoples whose loyalty to tribe and community reigns over their commitment to the rule of law. The marking of belonging to the realm of culture and religion, as opposed to the realm of law and reason, has devastating consequences. . . . [T]he West has often defined the benefits of modernity to those it considers to be outside of it. Evicted from the universal, and thus from civilization and progress, the non-West occupies a zone outside the law. Violence may be directed at it with impunity. (Razack, 2007)

6. For a genealogy of the "human," see Sylvia Wynter's "Unsettling the Coloniality of Being/Power/Truth/Freedom: Towards the Human, After Man, Its Overrepresentation—An Argument." *CR: The New Centennial Review*, Vol. 3, No. 3 (Fall 2003): 257–337.

7. For more on this topic, see Walter D. Mignolo's essay, "Sylvia Wynter: What Does It Mean to Be Human?" in *Sylvia Wynter: On Being Human as Praxis* edited by Katherine McKittrick (Durham, N.C.: Duke University Press, 2015): 106–23. I also recommend Hasan Azad's interview with professor of anthropology Talal Asad in *Islamic Monthly* (October 20, 2015), in which Asad discusses the Eurocentric notions of "humanity" and "civilization" <http://theislamicmonthly.com/being-human-an-interview-with-talal-asad/>.

8. Deckha, *op. cit.*: 46.

9. Why Black Veganism Is More than Just Being Black and Vegan

1. This version of *Cut Piece* was the first version for a single performer. Yoko Ono. "Cut Piece." YouTube Video, 8:08, February 28, 2013 <https://www.youtube.com/watch?v=1YJ3dPwa2tI>. A lot of controversy surrounds the piece for obvious reasons, but some background on the controversy regarding the meaning of the work can be found at "Yoko Ono's CUT PIECE: From Text to Performance and Back Again" by Kevin Concannon, *Imagine Peace* <http://imaginepeace.com/archives/2680>.

10. Seven Reasons Why Labels Aren't Necessarily the Root of Oppression

1. Prince Ea. "I am NOT Black, You are NOT White," YouTube video, 4:35, November 2, 2015 <https://www.youtube.com/watch?v=q0qD2K2RWkc>.

2. Erica Pinto. "The Unequal Opportunity Race," YouTube video, 4:08, November 14, 2010 <https://www.youtube.com/watch?v=vX_Vzl-r8NY>.

3. Gazi Kodzo. "White People Stop Using Martin Luther King!" YouTube video, 6:11, March 4, 2015 <https://www.youtube.com/watch?v=Xvx6W9b9Ujo>. Kodzo describes the ways white people attempt to use benevolent images of black people to convince black people to be "peaceful." He says that white people are using Martin Luther King Jr.'s "peaceful" legacy as a "sedative for black people." Anytime white people get uncomfortable with black people's anger, they say "take your MLK pill."

11. We've Reclaimed Blackness: Now It's Time to Reclaim "The Animal"

1. Nelson Maldonado-Torres. "Rousseau and Fanon on Inequality and the Human Sciences," *CLR James Journal*, Vol 15, No. 1 (Spring 2009): 113–34 <https://globalstudies.trinity.duke.edu/wp-content/themes/cgsh/materials/events/reflections_Maldonado-Torres_respondent.pdf>.

2. Consider Carter G. Woodson's point, made in *History Is a Weapon: The Mis-education of the Negro*: "The same educational process which inspires and stimulates the oppressor with the thought that he is everything and has accomplished everything worthwhile, depresses and crushes at the same time the spark of genius in the Negro by making him feel that his race does not amount to much and never will measure up to the standards of other peoples" (see <www.historyisaweapon.com/defcon1/misedne.html>). Also see Demetrius L. Eudell's excellent chapter, "'Come on Kid, Let's Go Get the *Thing*': The Sociogenic Principle and the *Being* of Black/Human," in *Sylvia Wynter: On Being Human as Praxis* edited by Katherine McKittrick (Durham, N.C.: Duke University Press, 2015): 226–48.

3. Another notable exception from most discussions about anti-racist strategies is the superiority complex of many whites. Steve Biko notes: "It never occurred to the liberals that the integration they insisted upon as an effective way of opposing apartheid was impossible to achieve in South Africa. . . . One has to overhaul the whole system of South Africa before hoping to get black and white walking hand in hand to oppose a *common* enemy. As it is, both black and white walk into a hastily organised integrated circle carrying with them the seeds of destruction of that circle—their inferiority and superiority complexes." See Steve Biko, *I Write What I Like: Selected Writings* (University of Chicago Press, 2002): 64.

4. As quoted in Eudell, *op. cit.*: 229.

5. Notice how even *black people* will take on the frameworks of the white mainstream to discuss racism! I am not blaming Prince Ea; rather, I am drawing the reader's attention to how powerful white discourse is.

6. As quoted by Eudell, *op. cit.*: 227. Contrast this with views that suggest names/labels *do* matter and that part of self-determination is the power to give your population a name.

7. Representative movements include Negritude, Black Consciousness, Afrocentrism, Black Power, and so on.

8. I am borrowing Sylvia Wynter's wording from her must-read article, "On How We Mistook the Map for the Territory, and Reimprisoned Ourselves in Our Unbearable Wrongness of Being, of *Désêtre*: Black Studies toward the Human Project" in *Not Only the Master's Tools: African-American Studies in Theory and Practice* edited by Lewis R. Gordon and Jane Anna Gordon (Boulder, Colo.: Paradigm Publishers, 107–69). Anyone familiar with Wynter's work will notice that I am more hopeful about "black pride" movements, assuming we address the human–animal divide. Wynter would probably not consider this to be a meaningful step (especially given she never explicitly addresses the situation of nonhuman animals). Also, Wynter thinks that racism (and all other "isms") are merely functions of a grander territory. I agree with her, but think that discussing the human–animal divide helps us gain entry to that space. Still, I think she delivers a great critique in this piece and she remains influential on most of my views.

9. As quoted in Walter D. Mignolo's chapter "Sylvia Wynter: What Does It Mean to Be Human?" in McKittrick *op. cit.*

10. The two names that come to mind immediately are Jacques Derrida (with his discussion on animal traces) and Zipporah Weisberg, with her compelling view on animal repression.

11. For an interesting study on reappropriation projects in general, see "The Reappropriation of Stigmatizing Labels: Implications for Social Identity," Adam D. Galinsky, *et al* <http://faculty.wcas.northwestern.edu/bodenhausen/reapp.pdf>.

12. Notes from the Border of the Human–Animal Divide

1. Gloria Anzaldúa. *Borderlands: La Frontera, The New Mestiza* (San Francisco: Aunt Lute Books, 1987): 109.

2. Césaire's response to the charge that négritude is "essentialist" can be found in *The Oxford Encyclopedia for African Thought*, Vol. I, edited by Abiola Irele and Biodun Jeyifo (Oxford: Oxford University Press, 2001): 218.

3. I have similar thoughts about the expectation that we are all supposed to be pushing for animal "rights," when rights don't even protect most of *us*.

4. Jinthana Haritaworn discusses this issue in "Decolonizing the Non/Human" in *GLQ: A Journal of Lesbian and Gay Studies*, Vol. 21, Nos. 2–3 (June 2015): 210–13. Haritaworn argues that we have to place the interhuman

(people historically excluded from "humanity") alongside the inhuman in environmentalist discourse as opposed to maintaining the narrative that "humans are supposed to appropriately remain in the background—the protectors of a 'nature' that is decidedly nonhuman and must, if anything, be protected from humans that are marked as environmentally destructive." Haritaworn draws the reader's attention to the effects of extraction of resources, siting of hazardous facilities, and dumping of toxic wastes with respect to plant life and ecosystems, but notes that some humans, indigenous people, and the poor in particular, are massively impacted as well: "Those whose subjugating and overconsumptive stance to 'nature' causes the greatest pollution are not the ones who pay its price. Those who are paying it, meanwhile, are labeled anti-environmental." As a result, Haritaworn holds that "we need to go beyond a simple analytic of anthropocentrism."

5. María Lugones. "Toward a Decolonial Feminism," *Hypatia* Vol. 25, No. 4 (Fall 2010): 742.

6. A great place to start is with Linda Martín Alcoff's framing of the issue in "The Problem of Speaking for Others," in *Cultural Critique*, No. 20 (Winter, 1991–92): 5–32.

7. I am borrowing this wording from Zakiyyah Iman Jackson's summary of a quote by Aimé Césaire. See her excellent paper, "Animal: New Directions in the Theorization of Race and Posthumanism," *Feminist Studies*, Vol. 39, No. 3 (2013): 669–85 <https://www.jstor.org/stable/23719431?seq=1#page_scan_tab_contents>.

8. It's well worth noting that the few times non-white, non-male, etc. views or works make their way into "the canon," they tend to reaffirm or support the views already put forth by white, Western males. The few times I've been encouraged to reach beyond "the canon" in my field (philosophy), it was for the purpose of "maintaining diversity." So, it's a situation couched as: *Well, we are forced to have x percent of [always white] women and x percent of "minorities" on the syllabus . . . but make sure you use the theories of [white men] if you want your own work to be taken seriously.* I think there is a definite correlation between pretending the demographics of context don't matter and the process of making non-Western, non-white, non-male, etc. voices and views irrelevant. One way this might work is to sanitize problematic aspects of certain views

or traditions, thus making dissenting voices and positions not important and not worth hearing. Philosopher Charles W. Mills writes about this with respect to political philosophy in particular in "Modernity, Persons, and Subpersons," in *Race and the Foundations of Knowledge: Cultural Amnesia in the Academy* edited by Joseph A. Young and Jana Evans Braziel (Urbana: University of Illinois Press, 2006): 220:

> Apart from being—unlike the present narrative—true to the actual historical record, and so demanding implementation on those grounds alone, this transformation would have the great virtue of uniting the conceptual spaces and periodization times of the white political and the nonwhite political. Textbooks authorize an account of the history of Western political philosophy, which moves smoothly from Plato to Rawls without dealing with race, as if, in the modern period, Western theorists were proclaiming their egalitarian views as fully applicable to everybody. The West is constructed in such a way that racism and white racial domination have been no part of the history of the West, and the normative superiority of whites to nonwhites, justified by these theorists, has been no part of that history. A mystified account of political philosophy complements a mystified account of recent world history, in which the central role of imperialism and racial domination has been either sanitized or written out of the record altogether, so that the distinctive features of the political struggles of nonwhites (abolitionist, anti-colonial, anti-imperialist, anti-segregationist) vanish into a white darkness.

Another interesting way voices that are non-white, non-male, non-Western, etc. are made irrelevant has to do with standardizing white + Western + male voices, perspectives, interests and theories. In her post on the superb blog Exquisite Misogyny (www.exquisite-misogyny.com/2015/11/18/r-solnits-80-books-no-women-should-read/), Aurora Linnea comments on this phenomenon in literary spaces:

Rebecca Solnit (author of 2014's *Men Explain Things to Me*) wrote for Literary Hub this sweet and summary slaying of *Esquire*'s reading list of greatest hits from the misogynistic canon, that dungeon of muscular prose otherwise known as The Canon, plain-n-simple, since as we're aware "literature" is synonymous with "men's literature" while we girls gossip irrelevantly in the corner with our namby-pamby CHICK LIT.

13. Vegans of Color and Respectability Politics

1. In July 2014, Sean Bergin, a white reporter for News 12 television in New Jersey, was suspended after covering a story about anti-police sentiments in the black community. In his report, he said, "The underlying cause for all of this, of course: young black men growing up without fathers." See "Reporter Suspended, Could Lose Job Over What He Said about 'Young Black Men' Live on the Air," by Jason Howerton, *Blaze*, July 14, 2014.

14. We Can Avoid the Debate about Comparing Human and Animal Oppressions, if We Simply Make the Right Connections

1. Gloria Anzaldúa. *Borderlands: La Frontera, The New Mestiza* (San Francisco: Aunt Lute Books, 1987): 489.

2. I've noticed that this doesn't seem to be as big a problem among scholars in the context of academia and some citizen-intellectual collectives.

3. Ultimately, who does or does not get offended is an empirical matter—I can't "armchair" my way into determining such things. But I think it's striking that almost all emails I've received from self-identified-racialized/other marginalized people have been mostly supportive of what Aph and I are doing, even if they are not vegan, and specifically overwhelmingly supportive of the ideas I've been developing in this space and with my dissertation. It's equally striking that the only emails I've received that indicate some sort of felt offense are from people who do not like the fact that I am adding humans to this presumably animals-only space.

4. Of course, if animals themselves were to organize into their own space and decide how they wanted to theorize and take charge of their liberatory efforts, this would not necessarily mean they were encouraging a gap between understanding their oppression and those suffered by humans. But

since it is we who are theorizing and taking charge on their behalf, I think the observation I've made about there being an encouragement of a gap is correct.

5. Walter D. Mignolo. "Who Speaks for the 'Human' in Human Rights?" *Human Rights in Latin American and Iberian Cultures*, Hispanic Issues Online 5.1 (2009): 7–24 <https://conservancy.umn.edu/bitstream/handle/11299/182855/hiol_05_01_mignolo_who_speaks_for_the_22human22_in_22human_rights22.pdf>.

6. There are some exceptions, I'm happy to say. But it's quite telling that there are demands for "decolonizing" critical animal studies. For instance, in June 2016 there was a fantastic lineup of speakers as well as other events at the University of Alberta Cripping and Decolonizing Critical Animal Studies conference/gathering. For more on this, visit <http:///www.kellysmontford.com/program>.

7. I've oversimplified the author's claim to keep things straightforward and focused on the subject at hand. Also, to be fair to the author, she was specifically interested in the practice of eating meat, but not eating other humans. But given some remarks she made about slavery and the general concept of "animal" itself, I think there was something "off" about a few things she said.

8. Other oppressions are involved with these concepts as well. But since I was using racial oppression as an example throughout the essay, I just wanted to remain consistent (as well as avoid listing a string of "isms").

9. Surely, I'm not saying we shouldn't focus on animal or black suffering! My point is that that is not the place to locate the connection we ought be looking for. We can connect earlier on by setting together race and animality (which almost everyone gets as naturally going together). If we note that both groups are affected by the same oppression, one caused by falling short of reaching real human status, then these struggles are so intimately intertwined that there is no need to have to posit further and more superficial "connections." This is a way to bring these experiences together at the fundamental level without offensively asserting that there must be something worth comparing at other, more experiential levels. Maneesha Deckha does a nice job tying racialization to animality.

10. I'm not endorsing a "liberal" conception of time that suggests everything that comes next is a necessary improvement over what came before. Instead, I have something like this in mind:

> Instead of providing a pat narrative of a unified movement advocating for a single, clear demand, *Born in Flames* leaves us with the unexploded bomb—the possibility that we do not know, cannot know, where we are in the history of the transformations we seek, what impact our varying actions will have, and whether our divisions and splits will expand or dampen different forms of momentum. This film somehow shows us how no individual actor or group has a grasp of either the current conditions, the causes and effects of resistance, or the ultimate destination.

This quotation comes from page 3 of the dossier on Lizzie Borden's 1983 film *Born in Flames*. See Craig Willse and Dean Spade. "Introduction: We Are *Born in Flames*," in *Women & Performance: A Journal of Feminist Theory*, Vol. 23, No. 1 (2013): 1–5. I would like to thank the Global (In)Humanities reading group at Duke University for providing the dossier.

15. Why Animal Liberation Requires an Epistemological Revolution

1. Frantz Fanon. *Black Skin, White Masks* (New York: Grove Press, 1952).
2. *Tautological* means redundant: the same concept is repeated or stated in different phrases.
3. Celia Edell. "Are Feminists Morally Required to Be Vegetarian/Vegan?" YouTube video, 11:37, January 29, 2016 <https://www.youtube.com/watch?v=gX9YIagwWr0>. I don't necessarily think Edell's argument about the morality part is contentious as much as I think the whole entire framework is uncritical.
4. Aph Ko. "The Feminist Case for Veganism," *F Bomb*, March 2, 2016 <http://thefbomb.org/2016/03/the-feminist-case-for-veganism/>.
5. I am not suggesting that activists can't learn and grow throughout their careers. However, I'm merely pointing out a trend (especially within

mainstream feminist spaces) that *clearly* disregards animal oppression, partly because a lot of feminists don't know how to include it in their analyses or they don't think it really matters. This points to an even larger problem with the theory they're using to understand their *own* oppression, considering our oppression is overtly anchored to the human–animal divide. These popular analyses are celebrated by the mainstream precisely because they don't tamper with the comfortable frameworks people are already using.

6. I first saw this clip from *Here Comes Honey Boo Boo* when I was taking a PhD seminar in Feminist Surveillance Studies with Dr. Rachel Dubrofsky. One of my classmates (now Dr. Tasha Rennels) was writing a paper on this topic titled, "*Here Comes Honey Boo Boo*: A Cautionary Tale Starring White Working-class People." I remember we were analyzing this clip. At the time, I didn't have the analysis I currently do now, but looking back I see the ways that Alana is framed as being "subhuman" and "wild."

7. Someone on Facebook once commented under my piece and stated that rarely do vegans actually discuss sizeism within the context of animality, so I wanted to note that it's not coincidental that, in this particular scene, Miss Georgia is tall and slim (a marker of acceptable white femininity) and Alana as well as her mother Mama June are ridiculed quite often because of their larger size.

16. How Social Media Serves as a Digital Defibrillator for "the American Dream"

1. Veronica Wells. "'I Didn't Have Enough Money for a Cup of Coffee': Issa Rae and Her Journey to Awkward Black Girl" *Madamenoire*, January 15, 2013 <http://madamenoire.com/255157/i-didnt-have-enough-money-for-a-cup-of-coffee-issa-rae-and-her-journey-to-awkward-black-girl/>.

2. Jonathan Chew. "Half of Millennials Believe the American Dream Is Dead," *Fortune*, December 11, 2015 <http://fortune.com/2015/12/11/american-dream-millennials-dead/>.

3. Adele Peters. "The American Dream Is Dead: Here's Where It Went," *Co.Exist*, September 3, 2015 <www.fastcoexist.com/3049643/the-america-dream-is-dead-heres-where-it-went>.

4. Colin Stutz. "Rihanna Found Her 'Bitch Better Have My Money' Co-Star On Instagram," *Billboard*, July 6, 2015 <http://

www.billboard.com/articles/columns/pop-shop/6620203/
rihanna-sanam-bitch-better-have-my-money-co-star-instagram>.

5. Shahnaz Siganporia. "Vogue Meets Rihanna's Sidekick Sanam," *Vogue India,* July 9, 2015.

6. Lindsey Robertson. "Rihanna Found Her 'BBHMM' Henchwoman Thanks to Instagram," *Mashable,* July 6, 2015 <http://mashable.com/2015/07/06/rihanna-bbhmm-henchwoman-instagram/#I3wGQZK6OsqY>.

7. Tasbeeh Herwees. "When Rihanna Messages You on Instagram, You Answer: An Interview with BBHMM's Sanam," *VICE,* July 5, 2015 <https://www.vice.com/en_us/article/when-rihanna-messages-you-on-instagram-you-answer-an-interview-with-bbhmms-sanam>.

8. Evelyn M. Rusli. "Facebook Buys Instagram for $1 Billion," *New York Times,* April 9, 2012 <http://dealbook.nytimes.com/2012/04/09/facebook-buys-instagram-for-I-billion/?_r=0>

9. "Sharecropping," PBS <http://www.pbs.org/tpt/slavery-by-another-name/themes/sharecropping/>.

10. Doreen St. Felix. "Black Teens Are Breaking the Internet and Seeing None of the Profits," *Fader,* December 3, 2015 <http://www.thefader.com/2015/12/03/on-fleek-peaches-monroee-meechie-viral-vines>.

11. O'Connor Clare. "Inside One Woman Investor's Plan to Get Black Female Founders Funding," *Forbes,* February 17, 2016 <https://www.forbes.com/sites/clareoconnor/2016/02/17/inside-one-woman-investors-plan-to-get-black-female-founders-funding/#6799bIce5eeb>.

12. Feliks Garcia. "Buzzfeed Accused of 'Stealing Ideas' by YouTube Personality," *Independent,* June 30, 2016 <http://www.independent.co.uk/news/world/americas/buzzfeed-video-akilah-hughes-petiton-plagiarism-a7112936.html>.

13. Kat Blaque. "The Dark Side of Buzzfeed," June 30, 2016 <http://katblaque.com/buzzfeed-exploitation-eradication-and-exposure/>.

14. Julie Carrie Wong. "How the Tech Industry Is Exploiting Black Lives Matter," *Guardian,* July 12, 2016 <https://www.theguardian.com/us-news/2016/jul/12/black-lives-matter-marc-benioff-facebook-twitter-uber>.

15. Kat Lazo. "Feminism Isn't Dead, It's Gone Viral," *TEDxTalks,* November 21, 2013 <https://www.youtube.com/watch?v=NNpUxKSmeE4>.

16. George Joseph. "Exclusive: Feds Regularly Monitored Black Lives Matter Since Ferguson," *Intercept,* July 24, 2015 <https://theintercept.com/2015/07/24/documents-show-department-homeland-security-monitoring-black-lives-matter-since-ferguson/>.

17. Matt Cagle. "Facebook, Instagram, and Twitter Provided Data Access for a Surveillance Product Marketed to Target Activists of Color," American Civil Liberties Union of Northern California, October 11, 2016 <https://www.aclunc.org/blog/facebook-instagram-and-twitter-provided-data-access-surveillance-product-marketed-target>.

18. bell hooks. *Feminist Theory: From Margin to Center* (Boston: South End Press, 2000).

19. bell hooks. "Choosing the Margin as a Space of Radical Openness," in *Yearnings: Race, Gender and Cultural Politics* (Boston: South End Press): 149.

17. Revaluing the Human as a Way to Revalue the Animal

1. Nelson Maldonado-Torres. "The U.S. Elections, Ethnic Studies, and the University: A View from the Historically Disenfranchised," Foundation Frantz Fanon, November 24, 2016 <http://frantzfanonfoundation-fondationfrantzfanon.com/article2370.html>.

2. See Walter Mignolo's suggestion to "undo" and "redo" as decolonial praxis. I also want to add "do-with," since we cannot ignore the social structures that are in place. Walter D. Mignolo. "Delinking: The Rhetoric of Modernity, the Logic of Coloniality and the Grammar of De-coloniality," *Cultural Studies,* Vol. 21 No. 2 (March 2007): 449–514.

3. Bernard Williams' great paper touches on this is "The Human Prejudice," in *Philosophy as a Humanistic Discipline* edited by A. W. Moore (Princeton University Press, 2006): 137.

4. Peter Singer. "Unsanctifying Human Life," in *Unsanctifying Human Life: Essays on Ethics* edited by Helga Kuhse (Oxford: Blackwell, 2002): 220.

5. For the record, I don't think Singer is saying this. What animal advocates are asking for is reasoning based on an emotional recognition of a "we" that includes animals *and* humans, since we all can suffer. What Singer—a utilitarian—is talking about is a calculation of interests in which we divorce ourselves from species membership in order to get the best objective result. It is worth noting that these are radically different positions.

6. There's another point that is often overlooked in discussions around speciesism. Views diverge drastically on this point due to different interpretations of what the human bond consists of. Following Singer, animal advocates' notion of humans preferring one another's interests does not even seem to be depicted as a "bond." Rather, it is portrayed much like an alliance between bullies. Their minds immediately leap to race and sex alliances that are problematic in nature. I always find it interesting that almost no one raises alternative race-and-sex alliances that are *not* problematic in nature. For instance, one can find the "help a brotha/sista out" mentality among communities of color, which encourages racial minorities to see problems affecting their people as more pressing and important than, say, the exact same problem affecting a white person. Or we can think of "sisterhoods" formed among women, in which women will provide physical, emotional, and financial support for each other and so privilege helping other women. Perhaps some people *do* think of these alternative cases as "racist" or "sexist." I think that this is as ridiculous as assuming spaces designed by women to be "women only," or spaces designed by and for people of color to be the equivalent of gentlemen's clubs or all-white and all-Christian country clubs. In the former, these bonds are formed as reactions to injustice whereas the latter are meant to *create* injustice.

7. Zakiyyah Jackson. "Animal: New Directions in the Theorization of Race and Posthumanism," *Feminist Studies*, Vol. 39, No. 3 (2013). Published online at <http://www.academia.edu/6169668/Animal_New_Directions_in_the_Theorization_of_Race_and_Posthumanism>.

8. I have in mind passages such as the following: first by Fanon, then by Wynter, quoted in *Sylvia Wynter: On Being Human as Praxis* edited by Katherine McKittrick (Durham, N.C.: Duke University Press, 2015): pages 13 and 1, respectively:

> What is by common consent called the human sciences have their own drama. . . . All these discoveries, all these inquiries lead only in one direction: to make man admit that he is nothing, absolutely nothing—and that he must put an end to the narcissism on which he relies in order to imagine that he is different from the other "animals." . . . This amounts to nothing more nor less than man's surrender. . . . Having

reflected on that, I grasp my narcissism with both hands and I turn my back on the degradation of those who would make man a mere [biological] mechanism.... And truly what is to be done is to set man free. (Frantz Fanon: *Black Skin, White Masks*)

Human beings are magical. Bios and Logos. Words made flesh, muscle and bone animated by hope and desire, belief materialized in deeds, deeds which crystallize our actualities.... And the maps of spring always have to be redrawn again, in undared form. (Sylvia Wynter: "The Pope Must Have Been Drunk, the King of Castile a Madman")

Drawing on such views, I am arguing in a forthcoming work that a biocentric rendering of "the human/humanity"—the idea that we are just another animal—*ensures* that we will never regard nonhuman animals as robust members of our moral community.

18. Black Veganism Revisited

1. See Steve Martinot and Jared Sexton's fine article on police violence as a "spectacle," "The Avant Garde of White Supremacy," *Social Identities* Vol. 9, No. 2 (June 2003), available at <https://www.ocf.berkeley.edu/~marto/avantguard.htm>.

2. The idea that oppressed humans, especially black people, and animals are supposed to remain a forbidden union when we think about social justice has always been one of the most dubious ideas out there. I think it works in the favor of those in power for us never to move past this fictional barrier and preserve this divide in discourse.

3. Walter D. Mignolo. "Delinking: The Rhetoric of Modernity, the Logic of Coloniality and the Grammar of De-coloniality," *Cultural Studies*, Vol. 21 No. 2 (March 2007): 449–514.

4. I borrow this wording from Sylvia Wynter.

19. Creating New Conceptual Architecture

1. Colorism is a type of prejudice based upon skin color wherein people of color who are darker skinned experience a unique subset of racism, and

people of color with lighter skin tones receive preferential treatment because of their approximation to whiteness. It is one of the most polarizing issues in the black community.

2. Roberto Ferdman. "The Disturbing Ways that Fast Food Chains Disporportionately Target Black Kids," *Washington Post*, November 12, 2014 <https://www.washingtonpost.com/news/wonk/wp/2014/11/12/the-disturbing-ways-that-fast-food-chains-disproportionately-target-black-kids/?utm_term=.192a0b0e47e9>.

3. Brande Victorian. "McDonald's to Honor Ava DuVernay, Marvin Sapp, Cousin Jeff and More at 12th Annual 365Black Awards," *Madamenoire*, June 24, 2015 <http://madamenoire.com/542336/365black-awards/>.

4. msstylesetter. "The Women of Afrofuturism Part I," *afrofuturistaffair* (Tumblr), June 16, 2016 <http://afrofuturistaffair.tumblr.com/post/53152938653/the-women-of-afrofuturism-part-I>.

5. Ytasha Womack. *Afrofuturism: The World of Black Sci-fi and Fantasy Culture* (Chicago Review Press, 2013): 24.

6. Frantz Fanon. *Black Skin, White Masks* (New York: Grove Press, 1952): 73.

7. James Baldwin appeared, alongside Martin Luther King Jr. and Malcolm X, on Henry Morgenthau III's Boston PBS public television show called *The Negro and the American Promise* in 1963. Baldwin stated: "What white people have to do is try and find out in their own hearts why it was necessary to have a nigger in the first place, because I'm not a nigger, I'm a man, but if you think I'm a nigger, it means you need it."

8. I had a Twitter conversation with Womack and another black woman in which we stated that black veganism is an Afrofuturistic praxis.

9. The Toni Morrison quotation is taken from a 1975 lecture on race, politics, and art. See August 28, 2014 <www.goddessblogs.com/2014/08/toni-morrisons-1975-lecture-on-race.html>.

10. Ytasha Womack, *op. cit.*: 42.

Afterword: *Carol J. Adams*

1. Mary Helen Washington. *The Other Blacklist: The African American Literary and Cultural Left of the 1950s* (New York: Columbia University Press, 2014): 3.

2. Henry Louis Gates Jr. *The Signifying Monkey: A Theory of Afro-American Literary Criticism* (New York and Oxford: Oxford University Press, 1988): 169.

3. Eric Foner. "Evolutionary Wars" (a review of *The Book that Changed America*), *New York Times Book Review,* January 22, 2017: 10.

4. Manisha Sinha. *The Slave's Cause: A History of Abolition* (New Haven, Conn.: Yale University Press, 2016): 586.

5. David Blight. *Race and Reunion: The Civil War in American Memory* (Cambridge: Harvard/Belknap, 2001): 4–5, and Blight, *American Oracle: The Civil War in the Civil Rights Era* (Cambridge: Harvard/Belknap, 2011): 21.

About the Authors

Aph Ko is a theorist and indie digital media producer, and founder of Black Vegans Rock, currently residing in Florida. She has a B.A. in Women's and Gender Studies and an M.A. in Communication/Media Studies. She is the co-editor of The Praxis of Justice in an Era of Black Lives Matter and served as the Associate Producer for the documentary film Always in Season.

Syl Ko studied philosophy at San Francisco State University and the University of North Carolina–Chapel Hill. She is currently working on a paper exploring Wittgensteinian "forms of life" defenses of animal use, taking into account the racialization of the animal.

About the Publisher

LANTERN BOOKS was founded in 1999 on the principle of living with a greater depth and commitment to the preservation of the natural world. In addition to publishing books on animal advocacy, vegetarianism, religion, and environmentalism, Lantern is dedicated to printing books in the US on recycled paper and saving resources in day-to-day operations. Lantern is honored to be a recipient of the highest standard in environmentally responsible publishing from the Green Press Initiative.

lanternbooks.com